THE MASKED MARVELS:
Baseball's Great Catchers

THE MASKED MARVELS:
Baseball's Great Catchers

*edited by Phyllis and
Zander Hollander*

◊ **Illustrated with photographs** ◊

A Zander Hollander Sports Book

Random House New York

Library of Congress Cataloging in Publication Data:
Main entry under title:

The Masked marvels.

"A Zander Hollander sports book."
  Contents: Introduction—Johnny Bench—Roy
Campanella—Ted Simmons—[etc.]
  1. Catchers (Baseball)—United States—Biography—
Juvenile literature. [1. Baseball players]
I. Hollander, Zander.
GV865.A1M34   796.357′092′2 [B] [920]   81-12182
ISBN: 0-394-85013-0 (pbk.); 0-394-95013-5 (lib. bdg.) AACR2

Photograph credits:
Malcolm W. Emmons, page 118; Nancy Hogue, page 36; Richard Pilling, pages 46, 61;
Carl Skalak, Jr., page 10; United Press International, pages 2, 14, 24, 26, 28, 40, 54, 66, 69,
79, 82, 86, 98, 104, 110, 124.

Manufactured in the United States of America   1 2 3 4 5 6 7 8 9 0

◊ *Acknowledgments* ◊

Baseball is a team game, and it was a team that produced *The Masked Marvels: Baseball's Great Catchers.*

The editors acknowledge with appreciation the contributions of Marty Appel, former New York Yankee publicist, who wrote the chapters on Elston Howard and Thurman Munson; Pete Alfano of *Newsday* (Johnny Bench and Yogi Berra); Ray Robinson of *Seventeen* (Mickey Cochrane); Joe Pollack of the *St. Louis Post-Dispatch* (Ted Simmons); Dennis Lyons of the Mamaroneck, New York, *Daily Times* (Gabby Hartnett and Joe Torre); Martin Lader of United Press International (Roy Campanella); and freelancer Ed Kiersh (Carlton Fisk).

Contents

Introduction

WANTED: A player able and willing to withstand constant crouching; wear heavy equipment in sweltering heat; survive the impact of a foul tip or a rocketing fastball on the mask; pounce on bunts; throw split-second strikes to any base; serve as a barrier between the spikes of a runner and home plate.

Wherever baseball is played—from the Little Leagues to the big leagues—there are always Help Wanted ads for catchers. There are not many volunteers.

Ever since the birth of baseball more than a century ago, most youngsters have wanted to be pitchers. It's the most glamorous position, the one that has the greatest influence on the game.

But every pitcher needs a catcher, the brave and bold one behind the bat. He knows he runs the risk of countless injuries, from fractured fingers to dislocated shoulders. But there are rewards that go with his position. He is the take-charge guy who calls the pitches and draws salutes from those men who depend on him.

The very best catchers, like the best players at any position, usually end up in the Baseball Hall of Fame in Cooperstown, New York. And among the 10 catchers profiled in this book are Hall of Famers Roy Campanella, Yogi Berra, Mickey Cochrane, and Gabby Hartnett.

Included also are Thurman Munson, Elston Howard, Joe Torre, and current catchers Johnny Bench, Carlton Fisk, and Ted Simmons—all of whom have made their special marks behind the plate.

The catchers profiled by no means represent all of the great catchers. No list would be complete without mention of Hall of Famers Bill Dickey, Ray Schalk, Al Lopez, Roger Bresnahan, Josh Gibson, and Mike (King) Kelly.

Bresnahan, as a New York Giant in 1907, was the first to wear shin guards outside his uniform. Gibson was considered the most awesome hitter in the black leagues, which existed before the majors admitted black players. Kelly, playing for the Chicago White Stockings in the 1890s, was credited with developing the hook slide that inspired a famous song of the day, "Slide, Kelly, Slide."

Oldtimers and rising stars, these skilled athletes took on the challenge of the position and became baseball's Masked Marvels.

—Phyllis and Zander Hollander,
Millerton, New York

THE MASKED MARVELS:
Baseball's Great Catchers

Johnny Bench nails Oakland's Dick Green at the plate in the 1972 World Series.

1

JOHNNY BENCH

◊ *Binger's Big Leaguer* ◊

He was only in the second grade but already daydreaming of the future. He liked to gaze out a classroom window and imagine himself a major leaguer. Even kids in small towns have big plans. And Johnny Bench was growing up in one of those towns—Binger, Oklahoma, with a population of 600. Binger was a long way from the major leagues, from the peanuts, popcorn, and Crackerjacks, from the stadiums that could hold the populations of a hundred little towns like Binger. It was 1952.

In his mind Johnny Bench could hear the crack of the bat and the fans cheering as if they were right outside the school. He could see himself driving the ball over the wall and circling the bases as his teammates waited to greet him. Other kids could dream of being

doctors, lawyers, firemen, policemen, and—
since this was Oklahoma—even cowboys, but
not Johnny.

"All right, children," the second-grade
teacher said one day. "What would you like to
be when you grow up?"

Seven-year-old Johnny Bench had big bright
eyes and high cheekbones that reflected his In-
dian (Choctaw) ancestry, and hands almost as
big as a catcher's mitt. He did not have to
search for an answer. "I'm going to be a professional baseball player," he said.

Ted Bench was the guiding force behind his
son. He was a truckdriver and furniture sales-
man in Binger, but he had once been a semiprofessional baseball player. He devoted himself to coaching Binger's 10-boy baseball
team—9 regulars and a substitute.

"Johnny was a pitcher," his father said. "He
won twenty-nine games and lost just once. But
the idea was that he'd become a catcher,
sooner or later."

Dad showed his son how to grip the ball
across the seams to get the greatest speed. He
taught him how to aim for targets like a belt
buckle, or the corner of the base, or the in-
fielder's knee. And he had Johnny throw twice
the distance a catcher normally throws to sec-

ond base. That made Johnny's arm even stronger.

When he was 12 years old, Johnny used to watch the big leaguers on television and take notes on their technique. And he read books on the famous catchers.

At Binger High he became the team leader and quickly proved that he was as effective in desperate situations off the field as he was on. There was the day the team bus lost its brakes on a tight turn, hit a guard rail, and flipped over. Johnny grabbed his nearest teammate, threw him to the floor, and fell on top of him. When ambulances reached the scene, two boys were dead and six were injured. Johnny was found unconscious, his foot sticking out the rear emergency door, but neither he nor the boy he fell on was seriously hurt.

By the time Bench was a high-school senior, the scouts and college recruiters were beating a path to Binger. Johnny was not only considered an excellent catching prospect, he had also gotten honorable mention on the high school All-American basketball squad. But Johnny never really gave any serious thought to playing college basketball. He was going to keep the pledge he had made in second grade to become a major leaguer.

He had to graduate from high school first, and that he did with the highest of honors—as valedictorian of the Binger Class of 1965.

Soon afterward 17-year-old Johnny was signed by the Cincinnati Reds. Because he was under age, his father had to sign the contract. Johnny received a small cash bonus and a $500-a-month salary. He packed his bags right away, said his good-byes, and headed for Tampa, home of the Reds' farm team in the Florida State League.

On his arrival at the Tampa airport, Bench was whisked away to Al Lopez Field, where a game was in progress. He would not have an opportunity to take in the scenery even that first night. He was told to get into uniform and report to the dugout. In the ninth inning, barely hours after he had left home, Bench was behind the plate, catching in his first professional game.

He hit .248 in 68 games at Tampa, and the following year, 1966, Bench moved up to the Reds' Peninsula farm team (in Hampton, Virginia) in the Carolina League. There he hit .294, batted in 68 runs, and clubbed 22 home runs in 98 games. He was an instant favorite of the fans, who honored him with a "Bench Night" on which they planned to shower him with a camera, record player, clothes, luggage, savings bonds, and other gifts. The only problem was that a thief broke into the storage room at the ball park and made off with everything.

Before the 1966 season was over, Bench moved up to Buffalo in the International League. In the very first inning of his first game, a foul tip—which every catcher dreads—fractured Bench's right thumb and sidelined him for the rest of the season. Indirectly, the fracture almost led to tragedy.

Bench returned home to Oklahoma to give his thumb a chance to heal. The Reds planned to use him in the Puerto Rican winter league so that he could pick up experience. But he almost didn't make it to Puerto Rico, or anywhere else. While in Binger, he was involved in a head-on auto accident. He needed 16 stitches to close a gash on his head and 14 more to close one on his shoulder.

"I didn't know how badly I was hurt, and I kept wondering whether I'd end up a cripple," Bench said. "Luckily, a doctor was in a car behind me and treated me until the ambulance arrived. He said that I was fortunate in being big-boned and strong; it could have been much worse."

After recovering from his injuries and returning to action in Puerto Rico, Johnny began the 1967 season in Buffalo. His big bat produced 23 homers, and his work behind the plate was such that one day in August, the Buffalo manager called John into his office and said, "I've got good news for you. They want you in the big league."

Indeed, the Reds had called up their prize prospect. He was only 19 years old.

The Reds' manager, Dave Bristol, sidelined the team's three other catchers—Johnny Edwards, Don Pavletich, and Jim Coker—and put Bench in the starting lineup. He played 26 games and batted just .163. But Bristol saw enough to know that Bench was there to stay.

At 6-foot-1 and 200 pounds, Bench had the type of body that could stand the abuse a catcher has to take. He was a confident, even cocky, receiver who knew how to handle pitchers. He could block the plate well, and he had a fabulous throwing arm.

Before the start of the 1968 season, Bristol showed his confidence in Bench when he traded Edwards to Houston. Bristol did open the season with Pavletich, but in the first week Pavletich was injured and Bench got his chance behind the plate. Nobody was going to get him out of there.

Bench caught in 154 games and batted .275. He hit 15 home runs and drove in 82 runs. He was named the National League's Rookie of the Year and also won the Gold Glove Award as the league's best defensive catcher.

He was praised by some of the biggest names in baseball. Willie Mays, the famous Giant outfielder, was annoyed that Bench was not named to the starting All-Star team. The Mets' Jerry Grote received most of the votes, which at that time were cast by the players. Later on the fans did the voting.

"The only reason they didn't give it to Bench was because he's a rookie," Mays said. "What's that got to do with it? You vote for the best, and Bench got my vote because he is the best and everyone knows it."

During spring training before the start of the 1969 season, Bench met Ted Williams, a Hall of Famer and one of the greatest hitters of all time. Williams was the new manager of the Washington Senators, and Bench wanted him to autograph a baseball.

"I've heard all about you, Johnny," Williams said. "You're a good one. You'll be a Hall of Famer for sure." Bench was speechless.

There were some observers, though, who thought the young catcher was too brash for his age. Some of the veteran pitchers on the Reds objected to the way he called a game. But Bench was only doing what a good catcher is

Bench has hit more home runs than any other catcher in big-league history.

supposed to do. He was taking charge. It did not matter how old he was.

"If you say what you think, you're called cocky," Bench said. "But if you have an objective in life, you shouldn't be afraid to stand up and say it. I want to be the greatest catcher ever to play the game."

Jim Maloney, one of the team's veteran pitchers, had several disagreements with Bench. But he respected the young catcher because of Bench's willingness to take on responsibility.

"Johnny will come out to the mound and chew me out as if I were a two-year-old," Maloney said. "But so help me, I like it. He has mastered a subtle skill in establishing a commanding personality."

What impressed his teammates was that Bench was not willing to rest on his abundant talent. He worked hard all the time, trying to improve. In his first two full seasons, for example, he had 32 passed balls—pitches that he should have caught and didn't. So Bench learned to handle low pitches. When he warmed up a Red pitcher before the game, he wore his full equipment and blocked any pitches that skipped into the dirt. In his third year he had just 3 passed balls in the first 100 games.

Bench was also maturing as a hitter. In both 1969 and 1970 he batted .293. It was in 1970 that he had 45 home runs and 148 runs batted in, was named the National League's Most Valuable Player (MVP), and led his team into the World Series against the Baltimore Orioles. The Orioles won the Series 4 games to 1, but Johnny knew he and his teammates would be back.

The Reds won the National League pennant again in 1972, only to lose to the Oakland Athletics in the World Series, 4 games to 3. Bench's all-around play, including 40 homers, brought him a second MVP award that year.

It was after the 1972 season that doctors found a growth on his right lung. The surgeons removed it, and fortunately the growth was found to be benign—not cancerous. While recovering, Bench received more than 15,000 get-well letters.

The mighty catcher came back almost as strong as ever, and in 1975 and 1976 he joined Pete Rose and Joe Morgan in leading the Big Red Machine to world championships.

The wear and tear on a catcher is never-ending, but despite numerous fractures and back and shoulder problems, Bench proved his durability as the years rolled on. In 1980 he tied Yankee Bill Dickey's career record of catching at least 100 games for 13 years in a row.

And it was in 1980 that the big boy from Binger hit his 314th homer, breaking Yogi Berra's career record for catchers.

As his father had said a quarter of a century earlier, Johnny wasn't meant to be a pitcher.

Campanella takes batting practice, more determined than ever after a knee injury kept him out of the 1955 All-Star Game.

2

ROY
CAMPANELLA
◇ *The Courageous Dodger* ◇

In the simplest terms, this was going to be the biggest game ever played in Brooklyn, a game that would reduce hardened professionals to humble tears, a game that would end a quest that had begun at the turn of the century.

Not only did it pack the usual tension of the seventh game of a World Series between two bitter rivals, but for the long-suffering fans who had been the butt of jokes about their beloved Bums, it was perhaps a last chance to rub the noses of the hated New York Yankees in the dirt. It was rumored that the Dodgers were moving out of Brooklyn.

Five times in the past the Brooklyn Dodgers had met the aristocratic Yankees in the World Series, and five times they had lived up to their nickname of Bums.

And so it had come as no surprise, a few days earlier, as the first breezes of autumn swept across New York in 1955, that the Yankees brushed aside the Dodgers in the opening two games of the Series.

In the solemn Dodger clubhouse, where no one dared raise his voice above a whisper following the second game, Jackie Robinson suddenly shouted to his teammates, "We've got to win this one. If we lose again, they'll be calling us choke-up guys the rest of our lives. Do we want that?"

A moment later a roly-poly man with a barrel chest and muscular arms stood up and said in an unexpectedly high-pitched voice, "Jackie's right. It's up to us to go out and get the job done. Let's go out and give 'em hell tomorrow."

The next afternoon, when the Series shifted to Brooklyn, the roly-poly man, Roy Campanella, was even better than his words. Campanella, who had once thought he'd never get a chance to play in organized ball because of his color, smacked a two-run homer in the first inning, then added a double and a single as the Dodgers won 8–3.

There was more of the same next day with Campanella again slugging a homer, a double, and a single to give Brooklyn an 8–5 victory. The teams then split the next two games, giving them 3 apiece and sending the World Series into the climactic seventh game at Yankee Stadium, a game that emotionally was a matter of life and death for the devoted Brooklyn fans.

It was the forty-ninth game ever to be played by a Brooklyn team in eight World Series, and the Dodgers were still trying for their first championship. For such great players as Roy Campanella, Jackie Robinson, Duke Snider, Gil Hodges, Pee Wee Reese, Don Newcombe, and Carl Furillo, it was the single game that could distinguish their careers and could give meaning to all they had given to Brooklyn.

A crowd of 62,465 people turned out in Yankee Stadium on October 4, 1955, and once again it was the round man with the high voice and explosive bat who made the difference and enabled the borough of Brooklyn to celebrate the greatest day in its history.

Although he had never hit well in the stadium, Campy delivered the first run of the game in the fourth inning when he doubled to left field with one out and came home on a single by Hodges.

In the sixth inning Campy was in the middle again when the Dodgers scored for the last time, laying down a key sacrifice bunt. When Elston Howard grounded to Reese for the final out of the game, giving the Dodgers a 2–0 triumph and their first World Series, Campy could be seen racing to the mound, where he grabbed pitcher Johnny Podres in a bearhug and lifted him high off the ground.

It was the grandest moment ever for both the Brooklyn Dodgers and Roy Campanella, and a month later it became even more special for Campy as he was voted the National League's Most Valuable Player for the third time. Only four times before then had a player been so honored with three MVP's, and Campy was joining such exclusive company as Stan Musial, Jimmie Foxx, Joe DiMaggio, and Yogi Berra.

A little more than two years later, Brooklyn no longer had a baseball team; the team had been moved to Los Angeles. Even sadder, Roy Campanella was fated to spend the rest of his life in a wheelchair, paralyzed, the victim of a frightful auto crash less than a mile from his home.

Campy was born on November 19, 1921, in Philadelphia. He was the youngest of four children of Ida, a black American, and John Campanella, a white Italian. Money was scarce, particularly during the Depression, but there was always enough food, since John Campanella sold fruits and vegetables.

Roy knew the meaning of hard work as a child. He would get up at 2:30 a.m. to help his brother Lawrence run a milk route, a job that paid Roy a quarter a day. Roy would go back to bed at 5:30, and by 8:00 he'd be on his way to school. He'd also help his father load his delivery truck, and had such other odd jobs as shining shoes, cutting lawns, and selling newspapers near Shibe Park, where the old Philadelphia Athletics used to play.

Even with work and school, there was always time for fun, and fun to Roy meant baseball. He was a good player, and when he was 10, in the Nicetown section of North Philadelphia, he was the only boy of his age allowed to play with the bigger guys.

There were few people in Nicetown who had money, and many of the boys didn't even have baseball gloves. The ball they used was beat-up and taped, and bats were cracked and had to be wired and taped. One time, when he was 11, Roy was catching and the mask he was using was too big for him. He took it off, and in the first inning a foul tip smashed into his face and broke his nose.

Roy's father didn't want him to play baseball, and whenever he had an injury, Roy would try to hide it. But you can't keep a broken nose a secret at the dinner table, and Roy's father made him promise not to play anymore. It was the kind of promise that wasn't meant to be kept.

As a kid, Roy pitched and played the outfield as well as caught. He had first been a catcher when he went to a tryout for a school team and saw that none of the other kids wanted to be catcher. By volunteering for that position, he knew he would always have a place to play.

At 15, Roy played for the Nicetown Giants, the only black team in the six-team Philadelphia sandlot league, and then Campy became the only black on his local American Legion team.

It was hard not to notice Campy then. He was big for his age, not so much tall as hefty, and he played ball like a man. In spring 1937 he joined the Bacharach Giants, a black semiprofessional team in Philadelphia. This involved traveling, which didn't please his mother, but she gave in when she learned that Roy would be paid $35 for two games. That was more money than her husband earned some weeks.

Roy played only one game with the Bacharach Giants before he was offered a chance to join the Baltimore Elite Giants of the Negro National League. That was the big leagues for blacks at a time when baseball was segregated—played only by whites. Black people, who then referred to themselves as colored or Negro, had their own leagues, and the pay was poor.

Roy was only 15. He was to earn $60 a month. The day after his sixteenth birthday, Roy quit school, feeling he was grown up enough to go into the world and earn his own way.

On St. Patrick's Day, 1938, Roy was packing to leave for his first spring training camp in Nashville, Tennessee. His mother came into his room and gave him a brand-new Bible. She said to him, "Whenever your mind is confused about something and your heart is troubled, turn to any page and start reading. Pretty quick you'll feel much better and stronger."

True to his mother's wishes, Roy always carried the Bible on road trips, even after he joined the Brooklyn Dodgers. He read it, believed in it, and drew strength from it.

In 1939 Campy became the Elite Giants' first-string catcher and they won the league championship, with Campy the hitting star.

That winter he played with the Caguas

team in the Puerto Rican League, and that was to be the pattern—summer ball in the United States, winter ball in Puerto Rico and Latin America—until 1945, when Campy played in an exhibition series against major-league stars.

Charlie Dressen, a coach with the Brooklyn Dodgers, followed Roy into the clubhouse and told him that Dodger president Branch Rickey wanted to meet with him the next morning. Roy came away from the meeting with the impression that Rickey was interested in him for a new Negro league.

But a week later Rickey and the Dodgers broke tradition with the historic signing of Jackie Robinson for their farm team at Montreal. Robinson was the first black player to break into white organized baseball. After Robinson came John Wright and Don Newcombe. And Campanella became the fourth black to sign a contract, in March 1946.

That season he was sent to Nashua, a Class B team in New Hampshire, with a salary of $185 a month.

With so much professional experience behind him, Campy quickly proved himself a standout at Nashua. He homered on opening day, and it wasn't long before the other players began looking up to him. Nashua won the New

England League championship, and Campanella was chosen Most Valuable Player.

There was another MVP award waiting for Campy at Montreal in 1947, leaving no question that he was ready for the majors. But Rickey wanted him to break the color barrier in the American Association. So Roy went to St. Paul, where in 35 games he hit 13 homers, drove in 39 runs, and had a batting average of .325, the kind of numbers that excited Leo Durocher, whose Dodgers were mired in a slump. Manager Durocher sent for Campy.

Roy arrived in the Brooklyn dugout on July 2, 1948, only two hours before a night game with the New York Giants. He was put into the lineup immediately.

His first time at bat, Campanella doubled, and later in the game he added two more hits. The next day he had a triple, two singles, and a walk, and in the final game of the series he smashed two home runs and a single. Campanella, who had been brought up as a third-string catcher, was soon the regular receiver.

Starting in 1949, Campanella caught in more than 100 games for a league record 9 consecutive years, enjoying a career that led to the Hall of Fame.

He had a career batting average of .276,

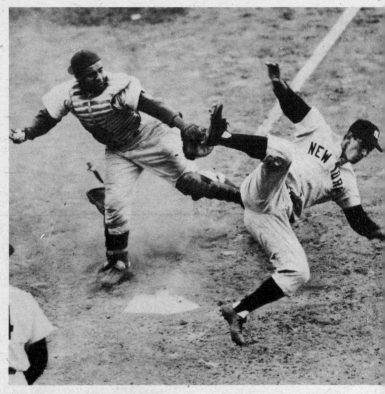

Roy Campanella's shin guard pops loose, but he holds the ball after tagging the Yankees' Billy Martin for the final out in the fourth game of the 1953 World Series.

clubbed 242 homers, and drove in 856 runs. In 1953 Campy set three major-league records for catchers, with 42 homers, 142 runs batted in, and 807 putouts.

Campanella was named the National League's MVP in 1951, 1953, and 1955, and he set a record by catching in 55 consecutive innings of All-Star Games.

Besides having many offensive skills, Campy was a remarkable defensive player, four times leading the league in fielding percentage. Despite his size, Campy was very quick behind the plate. He could pounce on bunts with the lightness of a cat, and he boasted a throwing arm that was both strong and accurate.

Being with the Dodgers also brought Campanella a lot of pain, both mental and physical. He suffered many injuries and often played while hurt. His teammates would beg him to bear down more on runners barreling into him at the plate, but Roy, ever the nice guy, didn't want to risk hurting someone else.

What became a real worry for him was the tough luck his team had. In 1950, for instance, Brooklyn lost the pennant on the last day of the season, and the next year the Dodgers lost a playoff to the Giants. Still, the Dodgers won five pennants in eight years.

Campy throws out the first ball to open the 1968 season at Shea Stadium. The Mets' Jerry Grote is the catcher.

Campanella was always a courageous player, a man who enjoyed baseball so much that he always seemed to do his best even after a crippling injury. After having surgery in 1954, he called the Dodger office and said to general manager Buzzie Bavasi, "You're talking to the Most Valuable Player in the National League for 1955."

He wasn't joking. Campy fought back with 32 homers, 107 RBI's, and a .318 average—and became the MVP.

Early in the morning of January 28, 1958, driving home and thinking about the Dodgers' move to Los Angeles, Roy skidded into a telephone pole in a rented car and broke his neck.

The accident that nearly cost him his life left him paralyzed from the chest down. But he was a deeply religious man, and he always had the ability to accept and adapt. When he wrote a book about his life, he called it *It's Good to Be Alive,* and he was able to say, "I have so many good memories. This is not really a bad one. I have accepted this wheelchair and I have accepted life."

Ted Simmons, always ready for the unexpected, recovers a high throw to tag Rich Hebner of the Pirates after Hebner fails to touch home plate.

3

TED SIMMONS

◇ *The Switch-Hitter* ◇

Ted Simmons grunted softly as he lowered himself into a squatting position behind home plate. It was August 14, 1971, and a warm, damp night in Pittsburgh's Three Rivers Stadium.

The St. Louis Cardinal catcher looked out to the mound where Bob (Gibby) Gibson, scowling fiercely, straightened his cap and hitched his trousers. Behind Simmons, the bulky figure of umpire Harry Wendelstedt leaned in as the Pirates' Willie Stargell scuffed his left foot deeper into the dirt of the batter's box.

The last two pitches had been popping fastballs, so the catcher signaled for a slider. Gibby rocked, threw. Simmons' mitt, knee-high on the outside corner of the plate, never moved as the ball rocketed home, slightly outside, then broke sharply into the strike zone. Stargell's bat never moved either, but the big right hand of Harry Wendelstedt flashed skyward.

"Strike three!" he bellowed.

Simmons leaped to his feet, raced toward the mound, waving the ball. A trace of a smile replaced the usual scowl on Gibson's face as they embraced. It was the Cardinal right-hander's first—and only—no-hitter, and the first to be caught in the majors by the second-year catcher. Gibson had recorded 10 strike-outs in the 11–0 rout, fanning the fearsome Stargell three times, while Simmons had contributed four hits to the Cardinal victory.

It was a long way from Highland Park, Michigan, in the suburbs of Detroit, where Ted Simmons was born on August 9, 1949, and where he grew up in the "good news, bad news" situation of being the youngest brother.

The youngest boy in a family is often disappointed when he is unable to do some of the things his brothers can do. But at the same time, he has those older brothers to help him, to teach him, to look out for him.

Ted's brothers, Jim and Ned, were very important in his development as an athlete because their father, a trainer of harness horses and a racetrack worker, put in long hours. But they were older—Jim was 14 and Ned 7 when Ted was born—and they often teased their kid brother.

And it's because of Jim and Ned that Ted became a switch-hitter. He was a natural left-handed hitter and an outstanding athlete on Detroit-area Little League teams, pitching and playing the outfield before settling in as a catcher.

But when he was 13, Jim decided that Ted would be an even better and more valuable athlete if he could hit from both sides of the plate. Like most 13-year-olds, Ted tried to kill every pitch. Jim was using a Wiffle ball, whose unsteady motion made it more difficult to hit, because Jim wanted to teach Ted to swing easily, to meet the ball, to keep his eye on it. Ted's anger would boil, and tears would come to his eyes. But he refused to give up.

Before he became a teenager, Ted was a Little League star. His team, the Southfield Giants, was undefeated for three straight seasons. To join the Giants, however, Ted quit another team, which strangely enough was managed by Russell Ellison, the man who would one day become Ted's father-in-law.

In his mid-teens Ted was a standout in the Detroit Amateur Baseball Federation, a sandlot league that sent many players to the majors, including Bernie Carbo, Ted Sizemore, Bill Freehan, and Willie Horton. Ted played on a team that not only won, but was also well fed. It was sponsored by the Kowalski Sausage and Bologna Company—and Ted's favorite lunch was a bologna sandwich.

At Southfield High School Ted was a three-sport star, attracting as many college recruiters as major-league scouts.

He was a quarterback, and later a running back, in football, winning second-team all-state honors as a senior. One night, against Royal Oak Kimball, he scored all of his team's touchdowns in a 28–24 loss, carrying the ball 30 times for more than 250 yards. In basketball he was a guard who averaged 20 points a game and one year led his team to the state finals, where it lost to Benton Harbor.

Ted was offered football scholarships to the University of Michigan, Michigan State, Purdue, Colorado, and other schools, and even paid a visit to Ohio State to talk with Woody Hayes, the legendary coach. But when Hayes learned that Ted, who weighed 187 pounds, was only a 10.3-second sprinter in the 100-yard dash, he said, "Tell you what to do. Put on twenty-five or thirty pounds, and you'll make a good pulling guard."

That was one of the reasons Ted decided

against the Ohio State Buckeyes and for the University of Michigan (Ann Arbor) Wolverines. Bob Hollway, then a member of the grid staff and later a National Football League coach, and Moby Benedict, the baseball coach, were the chief recruiters for Michigan.

By now, Ted was seeing a lot of his Southfield classmate Maryanne Ellison, but when she announced she would go to Michigan State in East Lansing to major in art, he went into action. After all, if Michigan could recruit him to play football and baseball, he could recruit her to study art. Maryanne was accepted at Michigan with a late-registration form that bore the stamp "in the interests of collegiate athletics."

Maryanne earned a degree from Michigan, and although Ted attended classes, he played neither baseball nor football there. Instead he turned professional. In 1967 the Cardinals chose Ted as their first pick in the baseball draft, making him the tenth player in the nation to be selected. Scout Mo Mozzali offered a package that included a $50,000 bonus, and Ted accepted. He promptly took $17,500 and bought a new house for his parents.

Even before he'd had his first class at Michigan, Ted was playing professional baseball. In the summer of 1967 he joined Sarasota, a Cardinal farm team in the Gulf Coast League. He hit .350 in only 6 games and was promoted to Cedar Rapids for the remainder of the summer, or until it was time to enroll at Michigan.

During his high-school years Ted had had a single interest—athletics. But as a college student during the protests of the late 1960s, he began to change, to grow, to become a man. He learned that there were more important things than the ability to hit a slider, and he began to think.

Still, there was baseball. His college classes and army-reserve duty meant that he would miss spring baseball training in his early years as a pro. He apparently didn't need it in 1968 when he starred in Modesto, in the California League, as Rookie of the Year, Most Valuable Player, and all-star catcher, leading the league with a .331 average and 117 runs batted in. He played his first games in St. Louis on weekends in September, went to college in Ann Arbor during the week, and was on hand to watch the Detroit Tigers beat the Cards in the World Series.

Ted's progress with the Cardinals continued. He moved to Tulsa, their top farm, in 1969, and again was Rookie of the Year with a .317 batting mark.

The Cardinals were obviously satisfied with

the young catcher, still a few months away from his twenty-first birthday. Shortly after the season ended, the Cards traded Tim McCarver, their first-string catcher for seven years, to the Philadelphia Phillies.

But there was another missed spring training—and another giant step—for Ted before he joined the big club to stay. To make up for the lack of spring work, he reported to Tulsa in May and played for three weeks, with a scorching .373 batting average, before moving up to the Cardinals just before the Memorial Day weekend.

The giant step? That was his marriage to Maryanne on May 2, 1970.

Exactly one month later he broke into the Cardinals' lineup, slammed a home run, and had a three-hit evening against the San Diego Padres. Two days later, catching against the Dodgers, he threw out his first base-runner, the speedy Willie Davis, and before the series ended he also pegged out Maury Wills and Willie Crawford on attempted steals.

Ted shared catching duties with Joe Torre in 1970. He played in 82 games and hit only .243. But he took over as first-stringer in 1971, with Torre playing third base. And Ted wound up with a .304 average. He made the All-Star team in 1972, was rewarded with a two-year

Batting as a right-hander here, Simmons can hit left-handed, too.

contract for $75,000 in mid-summer, and batted .303—with 16 homers and 96 runs batted in.

Although he was gaining acceptance as a worthy big-league performer, he still had to win over many of the St. Louis fans. His teammates nicknamed him Simba because his long golden hair reminded them of a lion's mane, but the Busch Stadium patrons weren't all-approving. When he hit a home run, the fans cheered, "Way to go, Simba!" But when he looked at a third strike, or let a passed ball skip back to the screen, someone would shout, "Why can't ya get your hair cut so ya can see the ball, ya dirty hippie."

His statistics kept improving, and in 1975, when the Cubs' Bill Madlock won the National League batting title with .354, Ted was second at .332, with 16 homers and 100 runs batted in. In acknowledgment, Ted was given a three-year contract for $600,000.

The Cardinals changed managers in 1976, with Vern Rapp replacing Red Schoendienst. Rapp was thought of as a strict believer in short hair. Ted reported to training camp with shorter hair and said nothing about it. He had found that there were more important things in life.

With the help of his wife, Maryanne, Ted

had become a collector and lover of art, specializing in antiques and decorative arts of the eighteenth century. The Simmons family, which now included son Jon, prowled the Missouri countryside in the off-season, visiting auctions and museums. During the winter they were regulars at the St. Louis Art Museum, and during the summer Ted spent many spare hours at museums and galleries in other big-league cities.

When Ted was honored by the Missouri Athletic Club as St. Louis' top sports personality of 1977, he donated the $500 prize to the city's art museum. Later he was named to the museum's board of trustees.

Rapp was replaced as manager by Ken Boyer, and Boyer by Whitey Herzog. Ted kept hitting in the .300 bracket and driving in his 100 runs. The great Tom Seaver described him as "the toughest out I ever faced." He caught another no-hitter, by Bob Forsch against the Phillies in 1978, and it was the first no-hitter at home by a Cardinal since 1924.

In the late 1970s the Cardinals began experimenting with Simmons in the outfield and at first and third base. His fielding was not up to true major-league standards, and the fans responded by booing him.

It was apparent that manager Whitey Herzog, who had become general manager as well, was rebuilding the team. And as the result of a series of deals, Simmons wound up in Milwaukee with the Brewers for the 1981 season. In addition to an annual $640,000 salary, Milwaukee agreed to pay him $750,000 over a three-year period.

The American League Brewers knew they were getting a winner: Ted had been named an All-Star six times, had a career National League average of .298, and had hit 172 homers, the most ever by a switch-hitter in the National League.

He is thought of as the best catcher in the history of the St. Louis Cardinals, and that's a long history.

Thurman Munson gave his all to the Yankees.

4

THURMAN MUNSON
◊ *Oh Captain, My Captain* ◊

Thurman Munson, captain of the Yankees, was walking tall.

He was never the sort of man to brag, or to remind people of his accomplishments. But when he was feeling prideful, you could tell it by his walk.

On this sunny spring day in 1978, he was leading his wife, Diana, and their three small children out onto the runway of Teterboro Airport in New Jersey, some 20 miles from Yankee Stadium. He wanted to show them a special airplane. The Beechcraft Duke on the runway was his. As one of the best catchers in baseball, he could afford such a luxury.

The children were fascinated by the plane, and even Diana, who had had some doubts about buying it, thought it was beautiful.

41

"We've come a long way," Thurman told his wife, "a long way from my paper route in Canton."

Munson was born on June 7, 1947, in Canton, Ohio, long before it became the home of the Pro Football Hall of Fame. Though Thurman enjoyed all sports, he was most fond of baseball. He looked forward to playing in the Canton Little League, and spent as much time as he could practicing with his father.

His dad, Darrell Munson, was a truckdriver who had to be on the road for long stretches. Even when he was home and played ball with Thurman, it wasn't much fun for the boy. Darrell Munson considered himself to be a good player, and he wanted to prove that to his son. As a result their simple games of catch often became very competitive. If a ball would take a bad hop and give Thurman a bloody nose, his dad would keep right on playing, telling Thurman to ignore it.

Thurman filled his time with school, baseball, and a paper route, delivering the Canton *Repository* after school. He'd pedal his bicycle as fast as he could to cover the route so that he could join his friends on the baseball field.

One friend who could ride as fast as Thurman was a girl—Diana Dominick. They met in the sixth grade while both were serving as crossing guards. Thurman was too young to be interested in girls, but Diana was interested in him. She'd pedal after Thurman as he made the rounds on his paper route, and then go to watch him play ball.

Diana became his Number 1 rooter when they entered Lehman High School and Thurman became a star athlete. He was a shortstop on the baseball team, a linebacker and half-back in football, and a guard in basketball.

In his senior year Thurman batted .581 and was selected to Ohio's scholastic All-Star team. As he neared graduation, Thurman received many scholarship offers to play football in college, but he was determined to be a baseball player. He decided on a college near his home—Kent State in Kent, Ohio.

There he became a catcher. His solid build was just right for that position, and from coach Moose Paskert he learned the finer points of catching. How well he did was evident when he was named to the college All-American team in 1968, his senior year. "When you consider that I've been chosen Number One from the thousands of catchers at colleges all over the country, this is quite an honor," Thurman said.

One of the many scouts who had watched

Thurman play at Kent State was the New York Yankees' Gene Woodling. He said in his report to the Yankees: "Get him."

In June 1968 the Yankees responded by making Munson their Number 1 draft pick, giving him a bonus of $75,000 and sending him to Binghamton, New York, in the Class AA Eastern League. His salary there was $500 a month.

The 1968 season was a big one for the rookie catcher on two counts: he batted .301 and in the fall he married Diana, his steady girl friend from sixth grade.

Thurman still had to serve in the Army Reserves, interrupting his 1969 season. He got to play only 28 games with the Syracuse Chiefs, the Yankees' farm team in the Class AAA International League. But the Yankees were impressed enough to call Munson up to the majors late in the season. Thurman caught in 26 games with the Yankees, and now he was ready to go all out in spring training in 1970.

The Yankees of the late 1960s were a disappointment. For a long time they had been baseball's most successful team, but between 1965 and 1969 they never figured in the pennant race. Thurman reported to Fort Lauderdale, Florida, and won the team's regular catching job.

But he started the season in a terrible slump. He had one hit in his first 30 times at bat, and he lost confidence. "I was sure I was going back to the minors," he said. "But Ralph Houk [the manager] called me in and said, 'Thurman, you're going to win a lot more games for me catching than hitting. So just relax and the hits will come.'"

In the next game Thurman collected three hits and was on the way to an outstanding season, in which he hit .302 and handled the pitching staff with the skill of a veteran. Moreover, the Yankees fooled the experts and finished in second place behind the Orioles. Later in the year the baseball writers honored Munson by electing him the American League's 1970 Rookie of the Year. He was the first catcher in league history to win the award.

Thurman soon became recognized as one of the best catchers in baseball. He was compared with Johnny Bench, the Cincinnati star, and with Carlton Fisk, who joined the Red Sox in 1972. Since the Yankees and Red Sox had always had an intense rivalry, it was natural that their two catching stars would become rivals.

But Thurman did not welcome the comparison with Fisk. He noted Fisk's frequent injuries and felt that his own good health was being overlooked by the press. It was just one of a list

Captain Munson was a leader at bat, behind the bat, and in the dugout.

of things about newspapermen that began to bother Munson.

Eventually he decided to have nothing to do with them at all. He refused to talk to reporters, and they had to turn elsewhere for interviews. Thurman felt they were always looking for controversy, and he wanted no part of that. By refusing to give interviews, Thurman didn't give the public a chance to know about him as a businessman or a family man. He preferred his privacy. His performance on the field could speak for itself.

As a businessman, he was a self-educated whiz at real estate. He bought shopping centers, apartments, and land to develop throughout Ohio. He made money on his investments, and he made money from the Yankees. His salary grew to over $300,000 a year.

As a family man, he found the love he had missed as a child. He and Diana had three children—two girls and a boy—and the time spent with them was important to him. Despite the demands of the baseball schedule, he was with them as often as possible.

Toward that goal, he asked the Yankees to trade him to Cleveland so that he could be closer to his home in Canton. But the Yankees wouldn't part with him. He was too valuable a player to trade.

Before the start of the 1976 season, after the Yankees had gone 12 years without a pennant, team owner George Steinbrenner and manager Billy Martin decided to name Thurman the captain of the Yankees. The team hadn't had a formal captain since Lou Gehrig, some 37 years before. George and Billy felt that Thurman would make the ideal captain as the New Yorkers began a new era in the freshly remodeled Yankee Stadium.

At first, being captain didn't mean that much to Thurman. "I was a player, not a fan," he said. "The history of the Yankees wasn't that important to me. I was never one to get caught up with tradition and that sort of thing."

But the more Thurman read about the Yankee sluggers—Babe Ruth, Gehrig, Joe DiMaggio, and Mickey Mantle—the more he developed pride in the Yankee uniform. For a hard-nosed competitor with a reputation for being a grouch, he was moved by the honor.

Thurman went on to enjoy his finest year in 1976. He batted .302 and drove in 105 runs as the Yankees easily won the pennant. And although they lost the World Series to Cincinnati, Thurman batted .529 in the Series, setting a record for the highest average ever by a player on a losing team.

That November the big call came to Thurman's home. He had been elected Most Valuable Player in the league, and by a substantial margin at that. Since the voters were all the sportswriters he didn't speak to, it was obvious that he had won it on his talent alone. He became the first Yankee ever to win both the Rookie of the Year and the Most Valuable Player awards.

Thurman should have been a happy man, but he wasn't. As captain, he found himself in the middle of a number of feuds among the Yankees, some involving himself and some not. When the Yankees signed Reggie Jackson for the 1977 season, the two did not get off to a good start. Reggie criticized Thurman in a magazine story even before the season opened.

Thurman feuded with owner George Steinbrenner over his contract. He continued to avoid the press. Between Fisk, Jackson, Steinbrenner, and the writers, his time at the ball park was not pleasant for him. He looked for an escape.

So in 1978 he bought the airplane. He'd taken lessons and gotten his pilot's license during the winter. Now he was able to be free of the ball park. Even after a late night game at Yankee Stadium, he would drive to the airport and fly home to Canton. He would spend the next day with his family, look after his business interests, and fly back for the next game. He enjoyed the routine. Alone in the dark sky, he felt peace and quiet.

As a man who always put the team ahead of himself, Thurman was proud of having captained the Yankees to three consecutive American League pennants in 1976, 1977, and 1978, and two consecutive world championships in 1977 and 1978. He could happily look back on a career in which he had batted .300 five times, driven in 100 or more runs in three straight seasons, and was selected to play in 7 All-Star Games. Although an injury had affected his throwing ability, he was such a master at calling pitches and running the game that he'd been awarded three Gold Gloves for fielding excellence.

He was now so aware of Yankee tradition that on Old-Timers' Day he asked his three great predecessors as Yankee catchers—Bill Dickey, Yogi Berra, and Elston Howard—to pose with him for a photo that he hung in his den at home.

Eventually his problems seemed to go away. A new contract from George Steinbrenner made him financially independent. He appreciated the contributions of Reggie Jackson on the field, and the two managed to patch things up. He still wasn't speaking to the press, but they had learned to respect him.

Thurman was able to show his tender side, too, even if it momentarily spoiled his grumpy image. One day in spring training, a sportswriter closer than the others to Thurman told him how he missed his children, who were back in New York, but couldn't afford to fly them down.

"Oh, I know that feeling," said Munson. "Here, take this money and fly them down here, but don't tell anybody I gave this to you."

In 1979 Thurman's success at the bat seemed to taper off a bit. The wear and tear of so many years of catching had taken its toll on his body.

Thurman began to experiment at first base and in the outfield. But close observers knew that he wasn't the player he had been. He was still valuable, and still a fine player, but the bumps and bruises were catching up with him.

That summer, after buying a new and more powerful plane—a Cessna Citation jet—Thurman flew home from Chicago to attend to some business and visit his family. He wouldn't have to be in New York for two days.

He was still getting used to the new aircraft, and on August 2 he took some friends to the

Akron/Canton airport to practice takeoffs and landings. But something went wrong that day.

At four o'clock in the afternoon George Steinbrenner received a call in his office at Yankee Stadium. It was from the airport in Canton. Thurman's plane had crashed. The captain of the Yankees was dead. He was 32 years old.

The news flashed across the country in minutes. Grief and sadness were felt by sports fans everywhere. Some remembered that the only other Yankee captain, Lou Gehrig, had died from a rare disease—amyotrophic lateral sclerosis. Others recalled the death of the great Pittsburgh Pirate star Roberto Clemente, who while flying as an airplane passenger had been killed in a crash several years earlier.

The Yankee team went to Canton for the funeral, and that night, back in New York, Thurman's friend Bobby Murcer hit a dramatic home run to win the game for the Yankees. Everyone in the Yankee dugout had tears in his eyes.

As time passed, people were able to ease their sadness and remember all the wonderful things about Thurman Munson.

His teammates remembered him as a man who liked people to think he was gruff, but who was really warm and generous, with a quick sense of humor.

His family remembered him as a loving husband and father who took time to pay attention to their needs, in spite of his busy schedule as a baseball player.

The writers had to admit that despite his surliness, he was an honest man who always let everyone know where he stood.

And the fans, who saw him only as a rough-and-tumble baseball player, knew him as a great talent who never gave less than 100 percent to his work.

He was a man of great character, and everyone in his or her way wished they had known him just a little bit better and a whole lot longer.

Teammates and fans rush to congratulate Carlton Fisk after he hit his game-winning home run against Cincinnati in the 1975 World Series.

5

CARLTON
FISK

◇ Farm Boy at Heart ◇

The ball seemed to hang in mid-air. Carlton
Fisk had driven a curve down the left-field
line, and as the ball soared toward the screen
atop Fenway Park's famed Green Monster (the
green left-field wall), over 35,000 fans rose
from their seats, screaming for a miracle. If
the ball stayed fair, the Boston Red Sox would
defeat the Cincinnati Reds in the twelfth
inning, and the 1975 World Series would be
deadlocked at 3 games apiece. But on this
cold October night in Boston, nothing was
certain.

Each time one of the teams had moved
ahead, the other had battled back. First Boston
had taken the lead, then Cincinnati, and with
the Red Sox trailing 6–3 in the ninth, a pinch-

homer by Bernie Carbo had sent the game into extra innings.

The stage was set for Fisk, the catcher affectionately called Pudge. The leadoff batter in the twelfth, he first looked at a fastball for a strike. Then came the loud WHOCK. Fisk had connected, and the ball became a white blur, sailing into the darkness above the lights. Would it stay fair? Fisk became a whirling demon on the first-base line, waving, spinning, and gyrating wildly, somehow hoping his body would force the ball fair. Finally the ball hit the pole atop the wall for a home run—and the crowd went berserk as the Red Sox won 7–6.

To Boston fans it was the greatest game ever played, and it wouldn't matter that the next day the Red Sox would lose the seventh game and the Series. Again, like so many times in the past, Pudge had been the hero.

The baseball season is a short one in the ice-and-snow country of New Hampshire. And when spring comes to the farming village of Charlestown, few people have time for games. Fences have to be mended, and barns usually need painting. It's rough work. But for Pudge Fisk, shoveling snow and milking cows was a stepping stone to the major leagues.

Born in nearby Bellows Falls, Vermont, and

then raised in Charlestown, Fisk was a chubby kid who had to be forced into shape. His strict parents expected the best from him, and farm chores were only part of his conditioning. Mrs. Fisk, who had played baseball herself as shortstop on a previously all-men's team, would often grab a fungo bat to hit Carlton grounders and flies.

But it was his father who was especially demanding. A natural athlete, especially good at tennis, Mr. Fisk was busy tending the farm and raising six children. When Carlton showed signs of having a "rifle arm" in high school, Cecil Fisk, in the grand New England tradition, became all fire and brimstone.

"It was just hard to please my dad," Carlton explained. "He always wanted more than a hundred percent. I once threw in forty points and grabbed a record thirty-six rebounds in a high-school basketball game. But did that satisfy my father? I'll never forget it. I came home and he said, 'You missed four out of six free throws.' Yet all that scolding served its point. In every area of life I became my own worst critic. I could always find something to improve upon."

Carlton played American Legion baseball and was spotted by a Red Sox scout named Irving Burns. "He had a good swing and a strong arm," said Burns, "and he could run like hell, but he had an awful lot of passed balls. To tell the truth, he didn't look that good as a catcher."

But Burns kept coming back to see him. One day somebody showed Burns a rock way out beyond left field at Bellows Falls. Somebody had painted on it that Carlton Fisk had hit a ball that far. "It must have been 450 feet from home plate," Burns said. "Anybody who could poke a ball that far had a chance."

Carlton decided to attend the University of New Hampshire on a basketball scholarship. He had visions of playing one day for the Boston Celtics. But the 6-foot-2, 210-pounder left college after his freshman year and trained his sights on baseball.

Chosen as the Red Sox's Number 1 draft choice in 1967, Fisk first had to go to the minor leagues for seasoning. During the next four years, while playing for such teams as Pawtucket (Rhode Island), Waterloo (Iowa), Pittsfield (Massachusetts), and Louisville (Kentucky), he had many trials with the Sox, but he never lasted beyond spring training. Disappointed so often, he was on the brink of returning to New Hampshire and the family farm.

Then came spring training, 1972, and the

baseball life of Pudge Fisk changed dramatically. His swing took on more authority. Balls started to soar over left-field walls. Coaches began to hear loud cracks from his bat.

One afternoon, as Fisk was taking batting practice, he checked his swing on a high, inside fastball. The ball bounced off his bat into his nose, breaking it. Fisk went down, but not out. Moments later he was up at bat again, taking his swings.

Manager Eddie Kasko was impressed with Fisk's attitude. And by the third game of the regular season, the 24-year-old Fisk had become the Red Sox's starting catcher.

Almost immediately the sturdy rookie was silencing the critics who had said, "The kid's a great glove, but only a streak hitter." For two months Fisk carried the team with his hitting. By mid-season he was batting .350, with 15 home runs, and he'd played in the All-Star Game.

But the Red Sox were floundering. And one day Fisk innocently told a sportswriter that veterans Carl Yastrzemski and Reggie Smith "are not lending inspiration to the team. They're supposed to lead the rest of us, but the younger players are taking over. When the veterans aren't aggressive or don't show desire, the whole team droops."

The quotes landed on the front page of every Boston newspaper, and all hell broke loose when Fisk checked into the clubhouse the next day. Rookies aren't supposed to mouth off that way. But an amazing thing happened. Smith and Yastrzemski started to hit—with a vengeance. From July to September the Sox staged a dramatic comeback, winning 50 of their last 65 games.

Manager Kasko nodded gratefully in the direction of his kid catcher.

It was a banner season for Carlton, named Rookie of the Year. He batted .293, with 22 home runs and 10 game-winning hits. And he ranked fourth in the voting for the league's Most Valuable Player award.

Despite the acclaim, Fisk remained a low-key, modest country boy. Other players became prima donnas. Not Fisk. Even in Fenway Park he never reacted to the fans, whose merciless boos often outweigh the cheers when a player slumps.

Off the field Fisk was equally reserved and conscious of his New Hampshire upbringing. He didn't smoke, and when other players would go out for a drink or two, Fisk preferred the privacy of his room. "Some guys have to work for a living," was his favorite line to get away from parties.

After signing with the Chicago White Sox in 1981, Fisk
is his old self as he puts the tag on Detroit's Lance Par-
rish.

This didn't mean that Fisk was a deadhead or a stuffed shirt who couldn't enjoy a good time. He had wit and a boyish charm.

His needs were simple. Rather than drive around in a $25,000 sports car or have an expensive wardrobe like many other superstars, Pudge was content with blue jeans, sneakers, and a small Pontiac.

"I'm never going to change," he said. "People are going to have to accept me for what I am—a farmer first, and a baseball player second." He repeated this to the ever-expanding hordes of journalists who followed him everywhere after his rookie season.

"New Hampshire and all that it means—the tractor, the corral, the trees, a big fire in the kitchen—make me the happiest guy alive," he said. "I can spend time with my wife and kids there, alone, without our privacy being bothered. If people don't like my ways or how I act off the field, so be it. I only ask that they respect me."

The entire league eventually did. But his second season, 1973, was a disappointment. A clear victim of the "sophomore jinx," Fisk saw his batting average dip 47 points to .246.

In 1974 he had turned things around and was batting .299 in June when he got an injury that nearly ended his career. As Fisk was waiting for a throw from the outfield in a game with Cleveland, Leron Lee ran into him. The rugged Fisk went down, his left knee badly damaged.

"One of the doctors who figured in the surgery told us that it would take a near miracle for Pudge to play again," said Fisk's wife, Linda.

But Fisk battled back, putting himself through a daily schedule of strenuous workouts. By 6 a.m. Fisk was pedaling 10 miles on an exercise bike and lifting weights. Then, to further rebuild his damaged knee, he ran, did pushups, and played racketball and full-court basketball.

Full of hope, he went to spring training in 1975. And broke his right arm. It was a staggering blow to Carlton, the Red Sox, and their rooters. He missed the first three months of the season, but came back spectacularly. Hitting a career high of .331, Fisk led the Sox to the pennant, slugged .417 in the playoff series, and capped it all with that World Series–tying home run against the Reds.

The following season was somewhat less dramatic. He hit only .255 and had just 58 runs batted in. Catching was wearing him down, and critics said that Fisk, then nearing 30, was past his prime. In 1977, though, he again bounced back. A leading contender for Most Valuable Player honors, Fisk raised his batting average to .315, pounded 26 homers, and had 102 RBI's.

Fisk had a respectable hitting record in 1978, but he developed arm trouble and came to a crossroads in his career. "I made a throw to second base in an exhibition game and it felt like a bullet had just exploded in my arm," said Fisk, who spent much of the 1979 season in the dugout and doctors' offices. He got to catch in only 39 games.

After seeing several specialists, Fisk learned that he had a bone irregularity—bone chips on the inner side of his elbow. Because of that, he asked to be moved to first base so he wouldn't have to do much throwing. But the Red Sox were well-stocked at that position and, once again, Fisk's future was cloudy.

Nonetheless, in 1980 he hit a resounding .289, with 18 homers in 131 games, and most people assumed that this confirmed New Englander would stay in Fenway Park.

But Fisk was getting fed up with the people who ran the only major-league team he'd ever known. By accident the Red Sox failed to mail his contract by the renewal date, and suddenly Fisk was declared a free agent. The Red Sox bid to keep him, but the White Sox made him an offer he couldn't refuse—a 5-year contract worth $2.9 million.

So, in 1981, a new phase began for the 33-year-old veteran of more than 1,000 games behind the bat.

On the very first day of the season, playing against his old teammates at Fenway Park, Fisk hit a home run to beat the Red Sox. The hometown fans cheered him. They had lost one of their favorites, and they wanted him to know it.

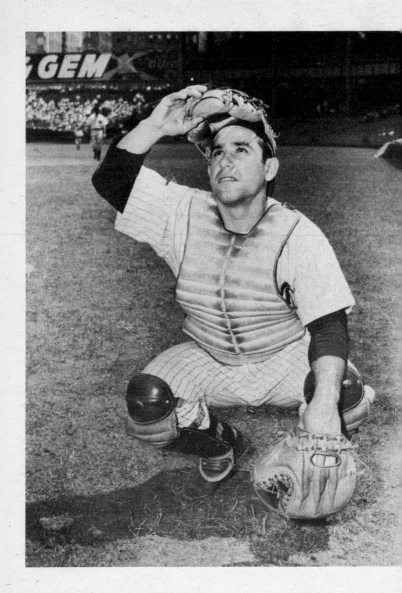

Yogi Berra, one of a kind.

6

YOGI
BERRA

◊ *No Laughing Matter* ◊

People who lived there called it the Hill, a
small lower-class section of St. Louis, a city
within a city. It was an Italian neighborhood,
and many of the modest homes had religious
statues resting on the neatly trimmed front
lawns. People lived and died on the Hill, but
the names always seemed to stay the same. A
father would pass his house on to his son, who
in turn would pass it on to *his* son. There was
no reason for Pietro Berra to suspect the same
ritual would not continue.

Pietro had come to the United States from a
small town near Milan, Italy. He had worked
at different jobs in California and Colorado
before settling down in St. Louis. He had come
to America to find a better way of life, and
when he got a permanent job at the La-

67

clede–Christy Clay Products Company, he sent for his wife, Paulina, who was still in Italy.

Although the Berras were in a new country, far from where they had been born, the St. Louis neighborhood made them feel comfortable. There were Italian restaurants, butchers, grocery stores, and bakeries. ALL THE SPAGHETTI YOU CAN EAT—AND MEATBALLS, $1 was a sign that made people on the Hill feel right at home.

Pietro and Paulina Berra had five children. The one they had the most difficulty understanding was Lawrence, who was born on May 12, 1925. His full name was Lawrence Peter Berra, although everyone at home called him Lawdie. From an early age Lawdie loved sports—football, soccer, and especially baseball. He would get together with his friends on Elizabeth Avenue and play in the schoolyard or in a small park nearby. Lawdie's best friend was Joey Garagiola, who lived at 5446 Elizabeth Avenue, across the street from the Berras.

When they were 10 and 11 years old, Lawdie and Joey helped organize a baseball club they called the Stags. They found a playing field at a local garbage dump. The kids cleaned up the area and measured off the bases. They used two old car wrecks as dugouts. The Stags were in business.

These are the Stags, Yogi's first organized team in St. Louis. Yogi's in the middle row, third from the left.

Pietro Berra did not care much for his son's preoccupation with baseball. He liked it even less when Lawdie came home with his clothing torn and his arms and face covered with dirt. The Berras did not have much money and they could rarely afford to buy their children new clothes. When Lawdie tore his pants, he was spanked.

Mrs. Beltrami, a neighbor, took the Stags to their first major-league game. They became members of the St. Louis Cardinals' knothole gang. Knothole gangs were formed by many major-league teams to promote baseball. The kids would get in free to the games or at a discount rate. "Knothole" comes from the early days of baseball when youngsters would watch a game by peeping through knotholes in the wooden fences.

When Lawdie and his friends turned 12, they joined a boys' league run by the YMCA. All the teams in the league wore uniforms except the Stags. They could not convince any of the businessmen on the Hill to sponsor them. So they wore their overalls and T-shirts, and some of them had to borrow gloves from the opposing team.

They may have looked shabby, but the Stags were a good team. Lawdie Berra and Joey

Garagiola were the leaders and best players. Lawdie played third base and second base, and sometimes he pitched. Joey was the catcher. The Stags finished second to a team sponsored by Edmonds Restaurant. The following year Lawdie and Joey were asked to join the Edmonds.

"Lawdie, you've got to study, you've got to get an education," Pietro Berra told his son. But Lawdie did not seem to hear. When he wasn't playing baseball, he was playing soccer, or roller hockey (using rolled-up newspapers as shoulder and hip pads), or football. He would practice tackling on the small strip of grass between the sidewalk and the curb.

At night Lawdie and his buddies would build a bonfire and roast potatoes. Or they would go down to Riva's Candy Store and play the pinball machine. On Sundays everyone went to church. Lawdie Berra knew that if he didn't go to church in the morning, his mother would not let him play ball in the afternoon.

Even though Pietro Berra encouraged his children to go to school, they also had to work at odd jobs to help the family pay the bills. "Are you going to deliver the newspaper like your brothers, or are you going to waste your time with this baseball?" Pietro asked his son.

Lawdie did not want any part of delivering newspapers. When he was 13, he became an amateur boxer at a local club. He earned $5 or $10 a fight and gave the money to his mother. It was a short career; he fought 9 bouts and won 8.

When he was 14, Lawdie decided he had had enough of school. He asked his mother and father if he could quit and go to work. Reluctantly they agreed.

But work wasn't much better. Or much fun. Lawdie worked in a coal yard wrapping blocks of coal that people on the Hill used to heat their homes. The job was okay, but at three o'clock every afternoon he would get the urge to join the other kids on the ball field. Every day Lawdie's mother would wrap a big hero sandwich in a newspaper for his lunch. Every day he would wrap his fielder's mitt in the newspaper, too. He left work early and went to play baseball.

Eventually he was fired, but he knew what he wanted. He would concentrate on baseball. He joined the Stockhams, an American Legion team on which his friend Joey Garagiola was playing. The team twice reached the semifinals of the Legion's national tournament.

Its manager was Jack McGuire, whose son

Jack, Jr., was the shortstop. One night Lawdie, Joey, and young Jack went to the movies. Before the feature film there was a short about India and its religious leaders, known as yogis. The film showed a yogi sitting in a meditating position—arms and legs folded, and looking very sad.

"Hey, Lawdie, you look just like that guy," Jack told Berra. "From now on I'm going to call you Yogi."

From that day on Lawrence Peter Berra became known as Yogi Berra.

The name seemed to fit. Yogi was short and squat, by no means a movie star. People even called him clumsy and ugly, and that hurt the shy young man. At least he knew he was a good ballplayer—better, in fact, than any other kid on the Hill.

The trouble was, not everyone else in St. Louis felt that Yogi Berra was the best player on the Hill. Joey Garagiola was the one the Cardinals offered a contract to. They gave him a $500 bonus to sign.

Branch Rickey was the Cardinals' general manager. He wasn't very impressed with Yogi. "The kid is too awkward," Rickey said. "He would never make it to the major leagues. He's a minor leaguer at best."

Disheartened, Yogi went to work for his brother Mike at the Johansen Shoe Company. At night he played ball in a semiprofessional league for $5 and $10 a game. Yogi wasn't aware that Leo Browne, who ran the American Legion post and was also a scout, had called George Weiss, the Yankees' general manager, and told him to come watch this unlikely looking player.

The Yankees were in St. Louis for the 1942 World Series. After the seventh game Yankee scout Johnny Schulte reached Yogi and offered him a contract. Yogi would receive $90 a month and a $500 bonus if he lasted the entire season with the Norfolk Tars of the Piedmont League. It was a deal.

For the first time in his 17 years, Yogi Berra was separated from his family. He joined Norfolk in spring 1943. Financially Yogi had a difficult time in this first year as a professional player. He wasn't making a lot of money, and most of what he made he spent. Yogi had a big appetite and was always hungry. He wrote home often, asking his mother for more money.

"Don't let your father know you're hungry," his mother wrote back. "Or he will make you come home."

He finally told manager Shaky Kain that he

would not play another game unless he got some extra money for food. "Okay, Yogi," Kain said. "Here's a couple of bucks."

Yogi filled up on hamburgers and soda, and that night he made six hits. The next day he made six more hits. In those two games he had 3 home runs and 23 runs batted in. He finished the season with a .253 average and 56 runs batted in. He also finished the season with a draft notice. World War II had begun, and Yogi the baseball player became Yogi the sailor.

Yogi didn't exactly look like the type of man the navy would want modeling its uniform on a recruiting poster. Nonetheless, he was a good sailor and saw action, serving on a rocket launcher. He was wounded during one battle, but Yogi did not want to accept the Purple Heart.

"My mother might think I got hurt or something," Yogi said.

Eventually he was transferred back to the States, to the New London submarine base in Connecticut. It was there that Yogi asked to play on the base team. The manager was Jimmy Gleeson, a lieutenant, who had played for the Cincinnati Reds before the war.

"Lieutenant Gleeson, I'd like to try out for the team," Yogi said. "I played for Norfolk last year. I hit pretty good, too. The Yankees own me."

"Aww, you don't look like any player," Gleeson said. "You look more like a wrestler."

Yogi convinced Gleeson he was really a professional player. After a few exhibition games, there was no doubt. When the base team played the New York Giants of the National League, Yogi made three hits.

Giants manager Mel Ott was impressed. He called owner Horace Stoneham. "See if you can buy this guy Berra from the Yankees," Ott told Stoneham. "They probably don't know how good he is."

Horace Stoneham tried, but Yankee president Larry MacPhail got suspicious. "Why are the Giants offering me $50,000 for this kid no one has ever heard of?" MacPhail wondered. He decided against any deal for Yogi.

On May 6, 1946, after Yogi was discharged from the navy, he was assigned to the Newark Bears, the Yankees' New Jersey farm team in the Class AAA International League. Yogi had an impressive season, batting .314 with 15 home runs and 59 RBI's in just 77 games. His roommate was Bobby Brown, a third baseman and aspiring medical student. When the International League playoffs ended, Brown and

Berra were called up by the Yankees to play in New York. The funny-looking kid from the Hill had finally reached the big time.

Yogi caught in seven games in the last week of the season. He batted .364 and hit a home run in his first game.

The Yankees had big plans for Yogi in 1947. They already had two other good catchers, Sherman Lollar and Aaron Robinson, but there had to be a place in the lineup for Yogi's bat. He was an unusual hitter, frequently going for bad pitches. Yogi could hit a wild pitch for a home run. But that didn't mean that pitchers dared throw the ball down the middle either.

Yogi was also gaining a fast reputation for his unique way of speaking. He would say the strangest things. At first they seemed funny, but when anyone thought about them, they usually made sense. For example, when he moved into his first home in Woodcliff Lake, New Jersey, Yogi said: "What a house, nothing but rooms."

Bobby Brown always got a kick out of the way Yogi phrased things. On a train trip once during spring training in 1947, Yogi was reading a comic book—his favorite literary matter—while Brown was reading a medical book. Both of them finished reading at the same time. "How did yours turn out?" Yogi asked Brown.

What the 1947 season proved, though, was that Yogi Berra's defensive skills were also laughable. He began the season in right field but did not distinguish himself. He was worse as a catcher.

In fact, he had the worst defensive record of any catcher in the majors. Yogi played because he could hit. He batted .280 with 11 home runs that year. And the Yankees beat their highly praised rivals, the Brooklyn Dodgers, in the World Series. But Dodger stars Pee Wee Reese and Jackie Robinson had a field day stealing bases against Yogi.

A determined Yogi Berra went home to St. Louis during the off-season and strengthened his arm tossing rocks in his backyard all winter. In 1948, when he raised his average to .305, Berra also showed some improvement defensively. But it wasn't until 1949 that he became a polished catcher. Casey Stengel had become the Yankees' manager, and he hired former Yankee catcher Bill Dickey as a coach. Dickey also became Berra's tutor.

Under Stengel, the Yankees continued their winning ways—and Berra was a major factor. He batted .277 with 20 home runs in 1949. In 1950 he hit .322 with 28 homers. In 1951 he

Short in build but swinging a tall bat, Yogi socked 358 home runs in regular-season play and hit the first pinch-hit homer in World Series history, in 1947.

batted .294 and belted 27 home runs. He was voted the American League's Most Valuable Player. And as in the previous two years, the Yankees were world champions.

In 1952 Yogi hit 30 home runs, a record for American League catchers, and the Yanks were champions again. They won their fifth consecutive world championship in 1953. By now Berra was an accomplished catcher. Stengel called him "my assistant manager."

He had an amazing memory and knew the strengths and weaknesses of the hitters of the opposing teams. He loved to talk to the hitters when they came to bat. It was partly on purpose. "Old Yogi," the Dodgers' Pee Wee Reese said. "He sure likes to distract you up there at the plate."

The Cleveland Indians ended the Yankees' streak of five straight pennants in 1954, but Berra won his second Most Valuable Player award. In 1955 the Yankees won the American League pennant again, and Yogi was named MVP for the third time.

In 1955, however, the Dodgers finally beat the Yankees in the World Series. The Yankees got revenge in the 1956 World Series when they beat the Dodgers in seven games. Yogi Berra took part in baseball history when he caught Don Larsen's perfect no-hitter in the sixth game. No one will forget the famous photograph of Berra leaping into Larsen's arms after Dale Mitchell struck out to end the game.

Yogi and the Yankees rolled on through the remainder of the 1950s, right into the early sixties. Yogi was named to the All-Star team 15 times. He played in 14 World Series. He wound up with 358 career home runs and drove in 100 or more runs in 6 different seasons.

Even when things were not going well for Yogi, he could always make people laugh. The reason he gave for the Yankees' losing the 1960 World Series to the Pittsburgh Pirates was, "We made too many wrong mistakes."

He was a success off the field, too, becoming the spokesman for a soft drink called Yoo-Hoo. He also owned a bowling alley with teammate Phil Rizzuto. By this time the easy-going, likable catcher and his wife, Carmen, had three sons, Lawrence, Tim, and Dale.

After the 1963 season, in which he rarely played, Yogi became the Yankees' manager in 1964. When asked why he expected to be a successful rookie manager, he answered, "You observe a lot by watching."

Yogi leaps for joy into the arms of Don Larsen, seconds after the Yankee right-hander pitched his perfect game in the 1956 World Series.

It did, however, turn out to be a trying year for the new manager. Critics complained that he wasn't tough enough. The players, they said, did not respect him as their boss. They considered him one of the guys.

Nonetheless, the Yankees won the pennant that year, only to lose to the Cardinals in the World Series. And Yogi was fired.

Berra, however, landed on his feet on the other side of town as a coach with the New York Mets. He rejoined his former boss Casey Stengel, the colorful old manager who helped distract attention from the worst team in baseball. The Mets improved over the years, and in 1969, with former Dodger Gil Hodges as manager, they became world champions. Yogi Berra, the first-base coach, had taken part in yet one more World Series.

Tragedy struck the Mets in 1972 when Hodges died in spring training of a heart attack. And Yogi was named manager. In his second season at the helm, 1973, he led an average Mets team from last place on September 1 into the National League playoffs, where they beat the Reds for the league pennant before losing to the Oakland A's in the World Series.

The miraculous comeback did not surprise Yogi. "You're not out of it, till you're out of it," he told reporters.

Yogi received another honor that year when he was voted into the Baseball Hall of Fame.

The Mets went downhill after that, and Berra lost his job in the summer of 1975. But nobody had to feel sorry for the kid from the Hill. He was welcomed back as a coach of the Yankees and was soon enjoying more championship seasons with the team that had been a winner with Yogi.

Mickey Cochrane liked to talk to the batters—and if
they listened, they'd end up striking out.

7

MICKEY COCHRANE

◇ *Tiger on the Loose* ◇

In the early 1920s, when baseball players traveled to Boston by train for their games, they often stopped at the Hotel Brunswick. The hotel was directly across the street from Boston University, where an undergraduate named Gordon Stanley (Mickey) Cochrane was studying business administration.

Mickey's piercing black eyes watched the celebrated baseball players come and go through the spring and summer months—Ty Cobb, Babe Ruth, Frankie Frisch, Walter Johnson, Rabbit Maranville, and many others. He'd read about all of them, and nobody could blame Mickey for being a little envious or for dreaming about the day that he, too, might become a major-league ballplayer.

Mickey's buddy, a student named Charlie

Farrell, who later became a silent-movie star, often joined him in the star gazing.

"These fellows have some great life," said Mickey to Charlie. "They go from one interesting city to another. I'm going to be one of them someday."

Mickey Cochrane was then in his late teens, a tough young Irishman with oversized ears, a square jaw, raven-black hair, and a muscular, unyielding body. He was close to 6 feet, weighed 180 pounds, and could do practically anything in sports.

He played outfield and third base for the Boston University (BU) baseball team and was an undefeated intercollegiate heavyweight boxer—in his one fight. In football he was a running back. Cochrane usually played football for 60 minutes, without a break. On one occasion he made a 52-yard field goal to win a game. When he wasn't busy playing baseball, football, or in the ring, Mickey also played basketball and ran in track events. Most observers rated him the best all-around athlete ever to attend BU.

The one fight that Mickey fought and won as a collegian shows his courage and competitive spirit. He was told that Rhode Island State had a heavyweight fighter weighing at least 250 pounds, and BU didn't have anyone to fight him. Mickey—according to the story, now something of a school legend—volunteered to represent his school in the ring and proceeded to knock his huge opponent flatter than a tablecloth.

This may have seemed an unlikely activity for a youngster with a literary bent, who enjoyed acting in plays by William Shakespeare and reading poetry by Rudyard Kipling.

Mickey was born in Bridgewater, Massachusetts, not far from Boston, on April 6, 1903, when Teddy Roosevelt was President of the United States. The son of John Cochrane, who made his living as a caretaker for a wealthy family in the neighborhood, Mickey learned the value of hard work and money early in his life. By the time he was in college, he was making his own way largely by playing saxophone in a jazz band, washing dishes in local restaurants, and ushering for $1.50 a night at the Boston Arena.

Eager to turn his tremendous athletic abilities into money for himself and his family, Mickey started to play professionally for the first time with a baseball team at Saranac Lake, in upper New York State. He later joined the Dover (Delaware) team in the Eastern Shore League. Because he was being paid, he played under the name of Frank King in order to keep his college amateur standing.

In Dover in 1923 he batted .327 in 65 games, with 5 home runs and 14 stolen bases. Although he wanted to play in the outfield, because that is where he thought he could best use his speed, he was asked by Dover's manager to catch, a position he had never played before.

It would be untruthful to say that Cochrane was born to the role. By the end of the season his body looked as if it had spent the summer in a torture chamber. He had cuts, bruises, and welts on his legs and arms. But he also had his pride and the knowledge that he had done remarkably well—so well, in fact, that by 1924 he was with minor-league Portland in the Pacific Coast League.

Tom Turner, owner of the Portland club, had personally scouted the young man and was determined to have him. It cost him $1,500, no small sum in those days, but Mickey delivered, batting .333, with 100 hits in 99 games, including 7 home runs.

Mickey, who was 21 years old, issued a challenge to Turner: "One summer is all I'm spending in the minors. Send me up to the majors or I'm quitting baseball."

Connie Mack, the respected manager of the

Philadelphia Athletics, who was a former catcher himself, made things easy. He bought the Portland franchise and then switched Cochrane to the Philadelphia roster in 1925.

Undaunted by the presence of Ralph (Cy) Perkins behind the plate, Mickey patiently waited for Mr. Mack to give him a chance in the starting lineup. Perkins was a team-spirited man who gladly acted as Mickey's mentor. He worked with his young disciple on the finer points of backing up first base, handling pitchers, blocking the plate, setting batters up, watching runners on the base paths, lunging for foul pops, and pouncing on bunts.

One day, with the A's trailing by a run, Mr. Mack sent Mickey in to bat for Perkins with two men on base and one out. Cochrane lined a double on the first pitch, two runs scored, and Mr. Mack had a new first-string catcher.

In that first year Mickey batted .331 with 139 hits and 6 home runs. But more than that, Mr. Mack was impressed with the quick intelligence of his new star. "I often matched his judgment with my own," Mr. Mack said. "I silently called for certain pitches from the dugout, without relaying my choices to Cochrane. And don't you know that that young fellow was usually doing exactly what I would have called for."

Mr. Mack was already assembling a championship team in those days of the mid-twenties. The key to it all was Cochrane—Black Mike to friends and foes alike. He became the receiver for the bullet-slinging Lefty Grove, whose temper was as mean as his left-handed fastballs. He handled the baffling right-handed curves of Moose Earnshaw and the left-handed slants of Rube Walberg, and he tamed the mysterious knuckleballs of Ed Rommel. These were the pitchers who led the way for Mr. Mack's team.

In his second season Mickey's average dipped to .273, but in 1927 he was up to .338 and was thought of as the best catcher in the game. Led by Cochrane, the A's won pennants for three years in a row and the world championship in two of them, 1929 and 1930. From 1928 to 1930, Mickey rang up averages of .331, .357, and .349.

Cochrane had always believed that catchers should do more than just catch and hit. They could also use verbal intimidation, and his role in the 1929 Series was a case in point. Mickey and his teammates became so abusive in their needling tactics that Judge Kenesaw Mountain Landis, baseball's commissioner, told them to stop such behavior, threatening to throw the culprits out of the game.

Always a hard man to restrain, especially when he believed he was in the right, Mickey tried to walk the fine line drawn by Landis. However, late in the last game, when a Chicago player seemed to be taking too much time in coming to bat, Cochrane screeched in a high-pitched voice, "Hustle it up, sweetheart! Tea will be served at four o'clock."

After the A's had polished off the Cubs for their championship victory, Landis visited the A's in their locker room. Off in a corner, still sweating from his efforts, Mickey grinned sheepishly at the commissioner.

"Yes," said Landis, as he sidled up to Mickey, "I heard you, sweetheart."

The A's faced the Cardinals in 1931 in a bruising seven-game Series. But this time a hawk-nosed man with as much dynamism in his legs as Mickey had in his bat, stole the Series for the Cardinals. That individual was John Leonard (Pepper) Martin, who in one week's time became a household word. Martin batted .500 and, while Mickey looked on with chagrin, swiped five bases. Cochrane always took full responsibility for Pepper's acts of highway robbery.

Cochrane had two more good seasons with Mr. Mack. But other things were happening off the field. The Great Depression was raging throughout America. Baseball attendance was down, unemployment was up, bread lines were long, and the stock market had fallen flat on its back. Mr. Mack had already been forced to sell off several of his stars, including Jimmy Dykes and Al Simmons.

Now, confronted with an offer from Detroit owner Frank Navin, lean old Mack, in desperate need of money for his franchise, decided to say good-bye to Cochrane. A deal was made that sent Mickey to Detroit for $100,000, an enormous amount of money in those troubled times.

Navin wanted to transform Cochrane into a player-manager—and that he did. The result, in 1934, was Detroit's first American League title in 25 years. Mickey, as everyone suspected he would, became an instant trend-setter. With his own performance showing the way, Cochrane molded the Tigers into a snarling, aggressive club that beat off the Yankees for the pennant. Hank Greenberg, Goose Goslin, Charlie Gehringer, Pete Fox, Marv Owen, and Jo-Jo White all did their share at bat and in the field, while Tommy Bridges, Schoolboy Rowe, and Alvin Crowder pumped their pitches into Mickey's big mitt. And Mickey won the American League's Most Valuable Player award.

At 31 years of age, Mickey sat at the top of the baseball world. However, the St. Louis Cardinals, featuring Pepper Martin and the Dean brothers, took the World Series in seven games. In 1935 the Tigers came back to defeat the Cubs in the World Series, and Mickey scored the winning run in the deciding sixth game. It was the first world championship for Detroit in history.

Sadly, the years following that triumph marked a decline in Mickey's fortunes, as well as those of his team. His physical and emotional health began to go downhill, and in May 1937 his playing career came to a sickening halt. Facing the Yankees' Bump Hadley at Yankee Stadium, Mickey seemed momentarily to lose sight of a Hadley pitch. It cracked into his left temple (there were no plastic helmets in those days), and he went down as if he'd been shot by a sniper. For 10 days Cochrane hovered between life and death. He did recover enough to manage the Tigers the next season.

In later years he did some coaching and scouting, and along the way he was elected to the Baseball Hall of Fame. His lifetime batting average was .320, with 119 home runs in 1,482 games.

When he died in 1962 at the age of 59, his

many fans were reminded of baseball historian Robert Smith's description of Mickey: "He was a man who would shout defiance into the face of an oncoming Sherman tank or would have snatched a baseball, if it happened to be in play, out of the mouth of a hungry tiger."

8

ELSTON HOWARD

◊ *The Pride of a Yankee* ◊

Elston Howard, the tall and muscular New York Yankee rookie, was nervous. It was tough enough for a rookie to make the team, but even tougher if that team had as many stars as the Yankees did.

This was spring training, 1955, in St. Petersburg, Florida. Each day Ellie would see the Yankee clubhouse man tap some players on the shoulder and tell them that Casey Stengel, the manager, wanted to talk with them. They knew at once what it meant; Casey was sending them back to the minor leagues.

The year before, as a hopeful outfielder, Ellie had gotten that tap on the shoulder and had been sent to Toronto. But the Yankees so liked his abilities, they had made him into a catcher. With instruction from Bill Dickey, a

97

Elston Howard confers with his first big-league manager, Casey Stengel.

one-time Yankee catching star who had become a coach, Ellie went off to Toronto in the Class AAA International League, where he batted .330 and won the league's Most Valuable Player award.

Now Elston felt that he had earned the right to play for the Yankees. As spring training neared its end, Elston was still with the team. The equipment trunks were packed and the team headed north, playing exhibitions on the way to opening day at Yankee Stadium.

When the Yankees arrived in Birmingham, Alabama, however, Elston was reminded why he wasn't just another rookie trying to make the team. In Birmingham he was told that a city law prohibited athletic contests between "racially mixed athletes." Blacks and whites couldn't play in Birmingham on the same field. Ellie didn't get to play that day.

If he was bitter, or if he was offended, he didn't show it. It wasn't his style. He was a man of great pride, and it was not part of his character to show anger at the injustice.

There were now less than two weeks to opening day, and the Yankees were down to three catchers—Yogi Berra, Charlie Silvera, and the rookie, Elston Howard.

There was no official announcement, no

clubhouse meeting, no congratulations from Casey Stengel. The final cuts were made, and Elston wasn't among them. He had made the club. He was the first black Yankee.

Ellie was 26, a trifle old for a rookie. He came from a segregated neighborhood in St. Louis called Compton Hill, where he was born on February 23, 1929. It wasn't far from the neighborhood where Yogi Berra and Joe Garagiola grew up.

As a youngster, Ellie was a sports fan and an admirer of Joe DiMaggio. In fact, Hawk, as Howard was known on the St. Louis sandlots because of his keen batting eye, copied DiMaggio's wide-open batting stance.

Ellie was a four-sport star at Vashon High School. He averaged 25 points per basketball game as a jump-shooting forward, and the team won 27 out of 28 games each of the two years he was on the squad. On the football team Ellie played end, kicked off, punted, and played defense. He threw the shot put and ran the quarter-mile for the track team.

Baseball wasn't a major sport at Vashon, and the team played only eight games. Ellie averaged .500 in hitting, and got more time in on the diamond with a semiprofessional team, the St. Louis Braves, for whom he caught and played first base. He played baseball when he wasn't working in Bauer's grocery store as an order filler or hauling bricks for a construction company.

As the only child of a college-educated dietitian and a high-school principal, Ellie knew the importance of a college education. He had many scholarship offers, but something happened in 1947 that played a major role in the decision Ellie had to make. It was in 1947 that Jackie Robinson, a rookie with the Brooklyn Dodgers, became the first black to play in the major leagues.

The majors hadn't offered Ellie a contract. He'd been to a tryout camp run by the St. Louis Cardinals, and wasn't cut until the final day. They said they'd get back to him.

Then the Kansas City Monarchs of the Negro American League offered Ellie a $2,500 bonus and a $500-a-month salary. "I decided to grab what lay under my nose and sign with the Monarchs," Ellie said. "I felt that with Robinson in the big leagues, things would be opening up for the rest of us. I'd have a chance to show what I could do with the Monarchs."

It was a chance for Ellie to experience life on the road and the same level of play as top minor-league baseball. Ellie wielded a big bat for the Monarchs, and the New York Yankees paid the Monarchs $15,000 for his contract in 1950. He was sent to Muskegon, Michigan, in the Class A Central League. Considered an outfielder at the time, he played in 54 games, batting .283.

A two-year stretch in the army—he was able to play baseball in Japan—caused Ellie to miss the 1951 and 1952 seasons. But he had a big year in 1953 with Kansas City in the Class AAA American Association, and an even bigger year in 1954 when he won the International League's Most Valuable Player award in Toronto.

It was after that MVP season that he married Arlene Henley, from his hometown in St. Louis. She was a bright, educated, attractive woman who would always be at Ellie's side, urging him on. When times were tough in the early years, she was a great support.

And times were tough. Because he was black, Elston could not stay at the same hotel with the rest of the Yankees in spring training. For years he had to live with black families in Florida. He wasn't welcome in all restaurants. As the only black player on the team, he could have felt very lonely, but he made friends easily and was well liked.

Phil Rizzuto, the veteran shortstop, was an early friend. He made sure that Elston never had to eat alone, and he'd often ask Ellie to join him for a late movie. Soon the seasoned Yankee stars, like Mickey Mantle, Whitey Ford, Yogi Berra, and Billy Martin, became his friends. He was simply one of the gang.

Casey Stengel brought Elston along slowly during his rookie season of 1955. He spent a lot of time in the outfield, and when Yogi needed a rest behind the plate, Ellie filled in. Despite Elston's irregular duty, he batted an impressive .290 in 97 games, belting 10 home runs. As a right-handed hitter in Yankee Stadium, he was never able to take full advantage of his power, for the left-field fences were very deep. So Ellie worked on his swing and learned to hit to right field more often.

The Yankees won the pennant in 1955, and Elston was ready for the World Series against the Brooklyn Dodgers. He started the first game in left field at Brooklyn's Ebbets Field. In the second inning, with Dodger ace Don Newcombe on the mound, Elston came to bat for the first time in a World Series. And he promptly blasted a home run to give the Yankees a 2–0 lead. He was only the second rookie in baseball history to accomplish such a feat.

The Yankees lost the Series, but Elston

Elston Howard complained only when he was sure he was right.

played every game. He played outfield, he caught, and occasionally he was called on to play first base. He was proving himself an invaluable all-around performer.

In the 1958 World Series the Milwaukee Braves and the Yankees were tied at two games each when Elston raced in from left field for a looping fly by Red Schoendienst. Ellie dove, caught the ball on his knees, and doubled the runner off first. It was the fielding play of the Series. The Yankees went on to win the Series, and Howard was named the outstanding player.

But it wasn't until 1961 that he became a regular at one position. Yogi Berra was moved to the outfield and Ellie became the team's Number 1 catcher.

It was a season to remember. Roger Maris hit 61 homers, Mickey Mantle hit 54, Whitey Ford won 25 games, and the man who caught for him, Ellie Howard, hit a sizzling .348 (plus 21 homers) to lead the Yankees—who went on to defeat Cincinnati in the World Series.

By now Howard was a year-round resident of the New York area, a popular and accomplished speaker to youth groups, and a respected player on all counts. He was one of the stars of the world-champion Yankees, and a player the younger ones looked to for advice.

Although he didn't approach his .348 average again, in many ways he enjoyed even better years after that. In 1963 he caught a grueling 135 games, led the league in fielding, batted .287, and hit a career high of 28 home runs. His day-after-day contributions to another Yankee pennant led the Baseball Writers' Association to elect him the American League's Most Valuable Player, the first black player ever so honored in the league.

"This is the high spot of my career, no doubt about it," said Ellie. "I've always been happy just to be a Yankee and to play with such great guys and get into all those World Series, but this just tops everything."

At age 34, he could still speak with the same enthusiasm for the game he had when he was a rookie.

It was probably not a coincidence that Ellie's last big year, 1964, was the last year of Yankee championship. Ellie hit .313 in 1964 and finished third in MVP voting behind Brooks Robinson and Mantle.

One by one all of Elston's famous teammates were traded or retired. By 1967 only Mantle and Howard remained from those outstanding teams of the 1950s. On August 3, with Elston batting only .196 and the Yankees in ninth place, manager Ralph Houk called him into his office.

"Ellie," he said, "you'll be shocked by this news, but if you think about it, you should be pleased. We've just traded you to the Boston Red Sox."

"Traded me?" Elston *was* shocked. After all, he was 38 years old, a Yankee for 13 years, and, if anything, near retirement. The thought of moving and starting over was not a pleasant one.

His first reaction was to retire and cancel the deal. His wife thought he had been treated very poorly by the Yankees. But when Tom Yawkey, the owner of the Red Sox, personally called Elston on the phone, he convinced him to come to Boston.

"We need you, Ellie," he said. "We're fighting for a pennant, we've got a young pitching staff, and we need your experience."

So Elston went, and put that experience to work. The Red Sox did win the pennant—their first in 21 years—and many gave credit to Ellie for his steadying influence down the final, frantic days of a thrilling race. And he was able to play in his tenth World Series.

Elston played for Boston for one more season, finishing up with a career average of .274. In that last season he invented the weighted "donut" used by hitters in the on-deck circle to make a bat feel light once it's removed.

Ellie wouldn't be out of work for long. The Yankees immediately hired him back for the 1969 season, making him the first black coach in the American League. He was to coach first base, work with young catchers, and serve as a batting coach, too. He wore his old number, 32, and was happy to return to New York.

Still, he hoped to become a manager. Bill Veeck, a baseball owner, tried to buy the Washington Senators in 1968, and would have hired Ellie as his manager, but he never acquired the team. Elston refused offers to manage in the minors or in winter ball in Latin America, feeling he had enough experience to manage in the big leagues.

In 1976 the Yankees returned to the top with their first of three pennants in a row. But in 1979 a circulatory problem forced Elston into the hospital for most of the season. Yankee owner George Steinbrenner made him a special assistant in the front office in 1980. He missed being on the field, but he enjoyed still being a part of the Yankee organization. Then a return of the health problem affected his heart, and he died on December 14 at the age of 51.

Elston had accomplished many firsts in his career. He was a man of dignity and class, and, as old teammate Whitey Ford put it, "He had courage early. Not even guys on our team realized how tough Elston had it."

Gabby Hartnett made his mark in Chicago as catcher and manager of the Cubs.

9

GABBY HARTNETT

◊ *Ol' Tomato Face* ◊

Darkness was quickly settling in over Wrigley Field in Chicago, paying no attention to the importance of the game going on below. The Pittsburgh Pirates and the Chicago Cubs were battling for the National League pennant, with the Cubs clinging to a half-game lead on the next-to-last day of the 1938 season.

The score was tied at 5–5 on this September afternoon, and Wrigley Field, then as now, did not have lights. So, after eight innings, the umpires decided to allow just one more inning before calling the game.

The Pirates went down one, two, three in the top of the ninth, and the first two Cub batters were also quickly retired. Up to the plate stepped Chicago's catcher and manager, Charles Leo (Gabby) Hartnett.

Pittsburgh pitcher Mace Brown looked as if he had things in control as the 37-year-old Hartnett, near the end of his playing career, swung and missed the first pitch and fouled off the second. It was so dark that Hartnett could barely see what he was swinging at.

The next pitch was a curve ball, and Gabby swung hard, sending it over the ivy-covered left-field wall. The 34,465 fans on hand went wild. The homer put the Cubs in first place, and the next day they clinched the pennant, beating the Pirates 10–1.

"I was really scared," Hartnett said in the clubhouse. "I got the feeling you get when the blood rushes to your head and you get dizzy. I knew the ball was gone the moment I hit it, and by the time I got to third base, I couldn't even see the bag for all the players and fans standing around it."

The road to what Hartnett would call his greatest day began in Woonsocket, Rhode Island, where he was born on December 20, 1900. His father was a streetcar conductor, and young Charles Leo was the first of 14 children raised in Millville, Massachusetts.

Hartnett, called Gabby by a sportswriter who found the young catcher very talkative, first caught the attention of organized baseball while he was working for a steel and wire mill in Worcester, Massachusetts, in 1920.

A scout named Jack Doyle, a former catcher whose crumpled fingers looked like a handful of peanuts, saw Gabby playing at a country fair and taught him some of his throwing techniques. Doyle picked out Hartnett because he liked the way Gabby held on to the ball one day when a big base-runner came charging into the plate and knocked him 20 feet. Gabby kept his grip on the ball and never said a word. The runner was out.

Hartnett got his first professional contract after a tryout with Jack Mack, who managed the Worcester (Massachusetts) team in the Eastern League. Gabby batted a modest .264 in 100 games.

Just before the season ended, he asked Mack to lend him two dollars so he could buy a steak. Mack handed him five dollars and said, "Send me some postcards from California."

"California?" a puzzled Hartnett asked. "What do you mean, California?"

"Why, that's where you'll be for spring training," Mack answered. "I've just sold you to the Chicago Cubs."

Gabby, also known as Ol' Tomato Face, because of the way his Irish face got bright red whenever he laughed, started out in the majors in 1922, catching for future Hall of Fame pitcher Grover Cleveland Alexander. He did not play often that year, though, because the Cubs already had an able starting catcher in Bob O'Farrell. Gabby got into just 31 games and batted only .194. But Alexander took a liking to the rookie and asked that Hartnett be his catcher whenever he pitched. From that point on, whenever anyone asked Gabby who the best pitcher he'd ever seen was, he always had the same answer—"Alexander."

O'Farrell remained the starting catcher in 1923, but Gabby saw a little more action, getting into 85 games and batting .268, with 8 home runs. And then, in 1924, manager Joe McCarthy made him the first-string catcher. Gabby responded by hitting .299 with 16 home runs and 67 runs batted in.

The next four years saw Gabby establish himself as a star receiver. In 1925, although the Cubs finished in last place, he batted .289, with 24 homers, and topped all National League catchers in putouts and assists. And in 1928 he reached the .300 mark for the first time, hitting .302 in 120 games.

The following year, 1929, America fell into the Great Depression, and Hartnett's career did likewise. In the Cubs' second spring training game, something snapped in his arm as he tried to throw a runner out at second. The Cubs would go on to win the 1929 National League pennant, but Gabby played in only 25 games, all but one of them as a pinch-hitter. With Zack Taylor behind the plate, the Cubs won the pennant by 10½ games.

As spring training approached in 1930, Gabby knew it could well be the turning point of his career. He remembered his pre-baseball years of working from 5:30 a.m. till 7:30 p.m. in the steel mills and was determined not to go back there.

"I remember one morning the temperature was twenty below when I set out for work," Hartnett said. "When I got to the plant, I discovered that both my ears had frozen. It was the greatest pain I'd ever known, and I vowed I'd never have to go through that again."

In 1930, enjoying his best year up to that point, Gabby hit .339, with 37 home runs and 122 RBI's, all career highs. He also led the National League catchers in fielding.

The 1930 Cubs fell to second place, and Joe McCarthy was replaced as manager by Rogers Hornsby. The Cubs didn't capture the pennant in 1931, partly because Gabby had an off year, hitting .282, with just 8 home runs. But in 1932, under player-manager Charlie Grimm, the Cubs were back in the World Series against Joe McCarthy's New York Yankees.

This was the Series in which Babe Ruth is supposed to have pointed to center field before hitting a home run against Charlie Root. Hartnett, who was catching, claimed it never happened.

"All Babe did was gesture and say, 'It only takes one to hit,' " Hartnett said. "He already had two strikes on him and was letting us know he still had another pitch."

Regardless of what happened, the Yankees swept the Series in 4 games, although Hartnett hit .313, with 5 hits, including a homer.

In 1933 Hartnett was honored with the starting catching position in the first All-Star Game. He was also the catcher the following year, when the Giants' Carl Hubbell struck out Babe Ruth, Lou Gehrig, Jimmie Foxx, Al Simmons, and Joe Cronin one after the other.

In 1935 the pitchers fared badly against Gabby. He hit .344 and led the Cubs to the World Series, which they lost in 6 games to the Tigers. It was the first of three straight seasons when Hartnett passed .300, and reached a peak in 1937 when he batted .354 as the Cubs finished second.

Midway through the 1938 season, Hartnett got a phone call from Cub owner Phil Wrigley.

"Gabby, we want you to manage the Cubs," Wrigley announced.

Delighted with the opportunity, Hartnett took the Cubs to win the pennant, highlighted by his dramatic home run. He stayed on as the Cubs' skipper through 1940, joined the New York Giants as a player-coach in 1941, and ended his 20-year playing career with 236 homers and a lifetime batting average of .297.

He was regarded as a brilliant catcher and an inspirational leader, and his achievements led to his election to baseball's Hall of Fame in 1955.

"There are two mementos of my career I wouldn't trade for anything," Ol' Tomato Face said shortly before he died at the age of 72. "My 1938 home-run ball and my Hall of Fame plaque."

As a hitter, Joe Torre could be counted on for power, especially in the clutch.

10

JOE TORRE

◊ *The Fat Boy Grows Up* ◊

"Boy, are you fat!"

The words stung the 15-year-old boy from Brooklyn, New York. He was too quiet and well mannered to answer back, but Joe Torre seethed inside. He was hurt because the man who spoke those words was Warren Spahn, one of his heroes, the star pitcher of the Milwaukee Braves.

It was July 1955, on a lazy summer day that had started out with great excitement for Joe. The Dodgers were still playing in Brooklyn, and Joe's older brother Frank had promised to take him to Ebbets Field for a game between the Dodgers and the Milwaukee Braves.

This wasn't just an ordinary case of a big brother taking his little brother to a baseball game. There was no need for them to wait in line for tickets. When they arrived at the ball park, they walked through a special gate marked "Players' Entrance" and went into the locker room and onto the field, because Joe's big brother was famous Frank Torre, first baseman of the Braves.

Joe was a big, chubby kid who loved his mother's Italian cooking almost as much as he loved playing baseball. Born on July 18, 1940, he was the son of a policeman and the youngest of five children. He was nine years younger than his big-league brother.

Joe's first glimpse of the life of a baseball player had come when he was 11 and Frank was playing for Denver in the minor leagues. With his mother, sister, and a cousin, Joe visited his brother.

"I brought my glove and they gave me a uniform," Joe said. "They let me work out with the team, and we lived at a big hotel. Before every game I had a steak, and after every game I had another steak. No kid ever had an experience like that."

Young Joe had a reputation of his own as a baseball player, both in high school at St. Francis Prep in Brooklyn and in summer ball with an amateur team called the Cadets. He could hit the ball hard and far, and a number of major-league scouts had come to watch him play. But they all went away with the same impression Braves' scout John (Honey) Russell had the first time he saw him.

"He sure could hit, but he was too fat and slow," Russell said. "I definitely wasn't interested in him."

But that day at Ebbets Field, things began to turn around for Joe. Spahn's biting comment about his weight, echoed by other Brave players, made Joe ashamed. After the game he wouldn't shower with the team because he didn't want them to see how fat he really was.

That night at dinner, brother Frank told him: "If you want to become a major-league ballplayer, you're going to have to lose weight. And instead of playing third base, you'd better become a catcher. Catchers are supposed to be big and husky."

Joe started watching his calories, and he talked the Cadets' coach, Jim McElroy, into letting him catch. Soon the weight began to drop—from 240 to 225—and Joe showed a natural ability at his new position.

"He had good hands, a fine arm, and lots of poise," said Honey Russell when he saw Joe catch for the first time. "And the catching helped his weight. He got thinner in the chest and still had as much power as any kid I'd ever seen."

By 1960 Russell had seen enough. He signed Joe to a professional baseball contract with the Braves. Torre received $15,000 for signing, quit his job as a page boy on the floor of the American Stock Exchange, and reported to the Braves' spring training complex in West Palm Beach, Florida.

When Joe, at age 20, arrived at the camp in 1960, there was muscle where there had been fat.

"When he walked into camp, I couldn't believe it," said Warren Spahn. "I couldn't believe it was the same fat kid I'd seen at Ebbets Field."

The Braves started Joe out at their Eau Claire, Wisconsin, farm team in the Class C Northern League. Catching every day, he led the league in hitting, with a .344 average, 16 home runs, and 74 runs batted in. What's more, he made just 9 errors in 117 games behind the plate.

In 1961 he got a big promotion to the Braves' top farm team, Louisville, of the Class AAA American Association. After 27 games Joe was hitting .342. But he was not fated to stay there much longer.

In Milwaukee, where the Braves played until moving to Atlanta in 1966, manager Charlie Dressen was worried. His veteran catcher, Del Crandall, had injured his arm. The Braves needed a healthy catcher.

Louisville was on the road, playing in Omaha, and Joe was asleep when the telephone rang in his hotel room at 1 a.m. It was Louisville manager Ben Geraghty, and he had a simple message.

"Joe, they want you in Milwaukee," Geraghty said. "You're going to the big leagues, and I don't ever expect to see you down here again."

Joe didn't waste any time getting to the airport. He caught a 3:30 a.m. flight to Chicago, then changed planes and flew to Cincinnati, where the Braves were playing the Reds. When he arrived, Dressen informed him he'd be catching both games of the next day's doubleheader.

Joe's start in the majors couldn't have been more exciting and productive. He caught both games; hit a single, a double, and a home run; and threw out three runners trying to steal.

Torre wound up catching 113 games his first year, batting .278, and hitting 10 home runs.

Like all catchers, Torre questions the umpire's call.

But Crandall was back in 1962, and as a result Torre got into only 80 games. He batted a respectable .282 but yearned for more action.

"I think I proved last year that I can play every day," Torre told manager Dressen. "I want to help this team win more than anything, and I can't do it from the bench."

The Braves agreed, and in 1963 Torre did most of the catching. He hit .293, belted 14 home runs, and was chosen for the National League All-Star team for the first of nine times. Then the Braves traded Crandall to the San Francisco Giants. There was no question about who was the Braves' Number 1 catcher.

In 1964 Joe had another outstanding season. He hit .321, with 20 homers and 109 RBI's. He was named the National League's starting catcher in the All-Star Game and was thought of by many as the best catcher in the majors. In 1965 Joe hit 27 home runs, with 36 in 1966, and the future couldn't have looked better for the 26-year-old power-hitter from Brooklyn.

But in spring training in 1967, Joe developed a sore shoulder. Then he twisted an ankle in a rundown play and was out for four weeks. After the season he had to be operated on to repair the damage to his ankle.

On opening day, 1968, a foul tip split his finger and he was out for another week. He returned for a night game against the Chicago Cubs. In the bottom of the first inning, Torre came to bat, with Hank Aaron on first base. As the pitcher was about to throw, Joe took his eyes off the ball for just a second to see if Aaron was running. And when he looked back, he couldn't see the ball. It crunched into his face, below the left cheekbone. Torre went down in tremendous pain and, after a few moments, he realized he couldn't see properly out of his left eye. It took him six weeks to recover.

"I was scared," Torre said. "When I came back, I was gun-shy. It was always on my mind. What if it happened again?"

Joe wound up batting only .271, with just 10 home runs and 55 RBI's that season. And in the final week he was benched. General manager Paul Richards publicly said that Torre had done little for the Braves the past two seasons. Torre was furious with Richards. And the inevitable happened. He was traded to the St. Louis Cardinals for first baseman Orlando Cepeda.

Just as on that day at Ebbets Field when Warren Spahn had told him he was too fat, the trade to the Cardinals proved a turning point in Joe's life. In 1969 he hit .289 with 18 home runs and 101 runs batted in. He both caught and played first base, and got his confidence back.

Shortly before the 1970 season, Cardinal manager Red Schoendienst came to Torre with an idea. The Cardinals had a problem at third base, because regular Mike Shannon was in the hospital with a kidney problem. What's more, there was a young minor-league catcher named Ted Simmons waiting in the wings.

"Joe," Schoendienst said, "I'd like you to give third base a try. You've got good hands, your weight is really down now, and I think you can do the job."

Although he hadn't played third base since high school, Joe took up the challenge and responded better than anybody expected he would. Now a slim 202 pounds, he played well there in 1970, hitting .325, with 21 home runs and 100 RBI's.

In 1971 the switch became complete. He made the All-Star team as the starting third baseman, batted an amazing .363, with 24 homers and 137 RBI's, and was named the National League's Most Valuable Player!

Torre remained the Cardinals' starting third baseman the next three years, and although he didn't approach his fantastic 1971 statistics after that, he never hit below .280 and was named to the National League All-Star team in 1972 and 1973.

After the 1974 season, at the age of 34, Torre came home, traded to the New York Mets for pitchers Ray Sadecki and Tommy Moore. Clearly at the end of his career, Torre managed to hit .270 for the Mets over the next two seasons and provided leadership to a young and struggling team.

It was those qualities of leadership that led to another big phone call in May 1977. It was from Joe McDonald, the Mets' general manager.

"Joe, we think it's time for us to make a move," McDonald said. "How would you feel about taking over as manager of the Mets?"

Torre responded to the challenge of taking over the last-place Mets. Since he had already struggled to lose weight and to learn how to catch and play third base and first base in the major leagues, Joe knew it would be a struggle to rebuild the Mets.

But little by little he began to mold the team in his own image. In 1980 he guided the Mets out of the National League East basement for the first time in three years and brought new hope for the Mets' return as contenders.

Torre had gone from being one of baseball's

great catchers to being one of the game's respected managers.

But in 1981 the Mets again finished under
.500 and the owners fired Torre. Nobody
doubted that Joe would be back again, manag-
ing another team. "I'm going to keep on doing
it," Joe promised, "until I get it right."

796.357 Masked marvels
Mas

DATE DUE
